Adobe® Integrated Runtime (AIR) for JavaScript Developers
Pocket Reference

Adobe® Integrated Runtime (AIR) for JavaScript Developers
Pocket Reference

Mike Chambers, Daniel Dura, and Kevin Hoyt

O'REILLY®

Beijing · Cambridge · Farnham · Köln · Paris · Sebastopol · Taipei · Tokyo

Adobe® Integrated Runtime (AIR) for JavaScript Developers Pocket Guide

by Mike Chambers, Daniel Dura, and Kevin Hoyt

Published by O'Reilly Media, Inc., 1005 Gravenstein Highway North,
Sebastopol, CA 95472.

O'Reilly books may be purchased for educational, business, or sales
promotional use. Online editions are also available for most titles
(*safari.oreilly.com*). For more information, contact our corporate/
institutional sales department: (800) 998-9938 or *corporate@oreilly.com*.

Editor: Steve Weiss
Production Editor: Philip Dangler
Copyeditor: Michele Filshie
Indexer: John Bickelhaupt

Cover Designer: Karen Montgomery
Interior Designer: David Futato
Ilustrators: Robert Romano and
  Jessamyn Read

Printing History:

June 2007: First Edition.

ISBN-10: 0-596-51519-7
ISBN-13: 978-0-596-51519-5
[T]   [8/07]

Contents

Preface

This book provides a quick introduction to developing applications for the public Beta 1 build of the Adobe Integrated Runtime (AIR). AIR, which prior to the Beta was referred to by its code name, Apollo, is a new cross-platform desktop application runtime being developed by Adobe. While Adobe AIR allows both Flash- and HTML-based application development, this book focuses on building AIR applications using HTML and JavaScript.

The book gives an overview of Adobe AIR, shows how to set up your development environment, and discusses new AIR functionality and APIs. Once you have finished reading this book, you should have a good understanding of what AIR is as well as how to build HTML and JavaScript applications for it.

AIR Runtime Naming Conventions

Adobe AIR allows developers to leverage a number of web technologies to deploy web applications to the desktop. Indeed, there are so many technologies, that it can be difficult to keep track of them all. Table P-1 lists the terms used in the book, and defines each one:

Table P-1. AIR runtime naming conventions

Name	Meaning
Adobe Integrated Runtime (AIR)	The cross-platform desktop runtime that enables the running of AIR applications.
AIR Application	An application built with Flash, HTML and/or PDF that runs on top of Adobe AIR.
Flash	Any content contained within a SWF 9 file format that runs in the Flash Player or AIR.
ActionScript	The ECMAScript-based programming language used to program Flash content. Unless otherwise noted, all references to ActionScript in this book refer to ActionScript 3.
HTML	Standard web-based markup language used to create and layout web pages.
JavaScript	Web-based implementation of ECMAScript used to program content within HTML applications.
PDF	Short for Portable Document Format, a technology that allows for seamless distribution and display of electronic documents.
Flex Framework	An XML and ActionScript-based Framework designed to make developing Flash-based rich Internet applications easy.
Flex Builder	An Eclipse-based IDE used to build Flash-based rich Internet applications using Flex and ActionScript.

What This Book Covers

This book gives a general overview of Adobe AIR, shows how to set up your development environment to start building applications, provides an overview of the HTML and JavaScript engines within AIR, and shows how to perform a number of common programming tasks within AIR.

As a general rule, features and functionality already in the Beta build are relatively stable and should not change radically (although they may be tweaked based on developer feedback). Any details discussed around unimplemented features and functionality are much more tentative and may change in future builds.

It is also important to note that the Beta 1 build of AIR is not feature complete, and a number of significant AIR features have not been implemented and/or included in the build.

The following is a partial list of features and functionality included in the Adobe AIR Beta 1:

- Mac support (OS X 10.4.8 and above; Intel and PPC)
- Windows support (Windows XP and Windows Vista Home Ultimate Edition)
- File I/O API
- SQLite embedded database
- All functionality within Flash Player 9, including complete network stack
- Windowing APIs
- Command-line tools (ADL and ADT)
- HTML within Flash content
- Top-level HTML applications
- ActionScript/JavaScript script bridging
- Flex Builder and Flex Framework support for authoring AIR application
- Application command-line arguments
- Drag and drop support
- Rich Clipboard access
- Native Menu API (Mac-only in Beta)
- Service Connectivity API
- File type association
- Application icons
- PDF support

Here is partial list of features planned for Adobe AIR 1.0, which are not included in Beta 1:

- Right-click and contextual menu control
- System notifications
- Flash content within HTML applications
- Support for additional versions of Microsoft Windows

We will highlight any features that we know may change in future builds.

What Beta Means

As discussed in the previous section, the Adobe AIR Beta 1 build is not feature complete, and some of the features are only partially implemented. Thus, the implementation of specific features or availability of any particular feature is subject to change between the Beta build and 1.0 release.

This also applies to the information within this book. The book was written at the same time that the Beta 1 build was being finalized and thus it is possible that some of the APIs or features may have changed between the time the book was completed and the time that the Beta build was finalized. This is particularly the case with API names. If something isn't working as the book suggests it should, make sure to check the online documentation, which will always have the latest information on the Beta 1 APIs.

You can find the latest information and documentation on AIR at:

http://www.adobe.com/go/air

You should also check the book's errata web site for the latest updates and corrections:

http://www.adobe.com/go/airjavascriptpocketguide

Audience for This Book

We hope this book is for you, but just to be sure, let's discuss some of the assumptions that we made, as well as what type of developers the book targets.

What Does This Book Assume?

The book assumes that the reader has at least a basic familiarity with creating HTML based web applications and content using HTML and JavaScript.

You should be familiar with web technologies such as HTML, JavaScript, Ajax, and CSS, as well as general web development concepts.

Who This Book Is For

This book is for developers interested in leveraging HTML and JavaScript to build and deploy applications to the desktop via the Adobe AIR. If you don't have any experience with developing with HTML and JavaScript, then we suggest that you spend some time getting up to speed on these technologies.

Who This Book Is Not For

While it is possible to create Flash and Flex-based applications with Beta 1 of AIR, this book does not go into any detail on Flash and Flex-focused AIR application development. If you are a Flash or Flex developer interested in building AIR applications, then this book can provide a good introduction and overview of AIR and its functionality, but you should view the AIR documentation and articles available from the AIR web site for a more Flash/Flex-focused discussion. You may also want to check out the *Adobe Apollo for Flex Developers Pocket Guide*, published by O'Reilly, which gives a Flex-focused overview of AIR.

How This Book Is Organized

This book contains the following chapters and appendixes:

Chapter 1, *Introduction to the Adobe Integrated Runtime (AIR)*
> Provides a general overview of what AIR is, and the types of applications it targets.

, *Getting Started with AIR Development*
> Covers tips on starting your AIR development, and the steps for creating your first AIR application.

Chapter 3, *Working with JavaScript and HTML Within AIR*
> Gives an overview of the HTML and JavaScript runtime environments within AIR, and provides an introduction to using JavaScript to access AIR functionality and APIs.

, *AIR Mini-Cookbook*
> Provides tips and tricks for accomplishing common tasks within AIR applications, presented in the O'Reilly Cookbook format.

Appendix A, *AIR Command-Line Tools*
> Lists AIR-specific command-line tools and their usage options.

, *AIR JavaScript Aliases*
> Lists JavaScript Aliases to Adobe AIR APIs

How to Use This Book

You can use this book both as an introduction to and overview of Adobe AIR, as well as a step-by-step guide to getting started with AIR application development. While it may be tempting to jump ahead to specific sections, it is strongly suggested that you at least read the first two chapters, which provide an overview of AIR, and discuss how to set up your development environment for building AIR applications.

This will make it much easier to then jump into the specific areas of AIR functionality that interest you.

Once you have read through the book and understand the basics of how to build an AIR application with HTML and JavaScript, then you can use the book as a reference, referring to specific sections when you need to know how to tackle a specific problem. In particular, the Cookbook sections should prove useful as you develop AIR applications.

Finally, this book is just an introduction to AIR and does not cover all of the features and functionality included within it. It is meant to complement, but not replace, the extensive and in-depth documentation on AIR provided by Adobe. Make sure to explore the AIR documentation in order to make sure you're familiar with all of the APIs and functionality not covered in this book.

Conventions Used in This Book

The following typographical conventions are used in this book:

Plain text
> Indicates menu titles, menu options, menu buttons, and keyboard accelerators (such as Alt and Ctrl).

Italic
> Indicates new terms, URLs, email addresses, filenames, file extensions, pathnames, directories, and Unix utilities.

`Constant width`
> Indicates commands, options, switches, variables, attributes, keys, functions, types, classes, namespaces, methods, modules, properties, parameters, values, objects, events, event handlers, XML tags, HTML tags, macros, the contents of files, or the output from commands.

Constant width bold

> Shows commands or other text that should be typed literally by the user.

Constant width italic

> Shows text that should be replaced with user-supplied values.

License and Code Examples

This work, including all text and code samples, is licensed under the Creative Commons Attribution-Noncommercial-Share Alike 3.0 License.

To view a copy of this license, visit *http://creativecommons. org/licenses/by-nc-sa/3.0/*; or, (b) send a letter to Creative Commons, 543 Howard Street, 5th Floor, San Francisco, California, 94105, USA.

You can find more information on Creative Commons at *http://www.creativecommons.org*.

Support and More Information

Accessing the Book Online

You can always find the latest information about this book, as well as download a free electronic version of it from the book's web site at:

> *http://www.adobe.com/go/airjavascriptpocketguide*

Online AIR Resources

Although AIR is a new technology, there are already a number of resources where you can find more information on AIR and Rich Internet Application (RIA) development.

Official AIR site

Primary web site for information, downloads, and documentation on AIR:

http://www.adobe.com/go/air

AIR Developer FAQ

Official AIR FAQ, answering common questions about AIR development:

http://www.adobe.com/go/airfaq

AIR Developer Center

Developer Center with articles, information, and resources on developing applications for AIR:

http://www.adobe.com/go/airdevcenter

AIR API Reference

AIR JavaScript API Reference:

http://www.adobe.com/go/airapi

AIR Documentation

Complete AIR documentation:

http://www.adobe.com/go/airdocs

AIR Forum

Official Adobe forum for discussing developing applications for AIR:

http://www.adobe.com/go/airforums

AIR coders mailing list

Mailing list for discussing AIR application development:

http://www.adobe.com/go/airlist

Mike Chambers' weblog

Mike Chambers' weblog. One of the authors of the book and a member of the AIR team who posts frequently on AIR:

http://www.adobe.com/go/mikechambers

MXNA AIR Smart Category

AIR Smart Category that lists any discussions about AIR within the Adobe online development community:

http://www.adobe.com/go/airmxna

Ajaxian.com

Ajax news site with information, tips, tricks and the latest news on developing with JavaScript and Ajax techniques.

http://www.ajaxian.com

YUI-Ext

JavaScript Library and Framework useful for building HTML- and JavaScript-based applications.

http://extjs.com

Flex Developer Center

Developer Center with articles, information, and resources on working with the Flex Framework:

http://www.adobe.com/go/flex2_devcenter

Flex coders mailing list

Popular mailing list for discussing development using the Flex Framework:

http://tech.groups.yahoo.com/group/flexcoders/

Universal Desktop Weblog

Ryan Stewart's weblog, which focuses on the latest developments in the world of RIAs:

http://blogs.zdnet.com/Stewart/

How to Contact Us

Please address comments and non-technical questions concerning this book to the publisher:

O'Reilly Media, Inc.
1005 Gravenstein Highway North
Sebastopol, CA 95472
800-998-9938 (in the United States or Canada)
707-829-0515 (international or local)
707-829-0104 (fax)

We have a web page for this book, where we list errata, examples, and any additional information. You can access this page at:

http://www.oreilly.com/catalog/9780596515195

For more information about our books, conferences, Resource Centers, and the O'Reilly Network, see our web site at:

http://www.oreilly.com

About the Authors

Mike Chambers

Mike Chambers has spent the last eight years building applications that target the Flash runtime. During that time, he has worked with numerous technologies including Flash, Generator, .NET, Central, Flex, and Ajax. He is currently the senior product manager for developer relations for Adobe

AIR. He has written and spoken extensively on Flash and rich Internet application development and is coauthor of *Adobe Apollo for Flex Developers Pocket Guide*, *Flash Enabled: Flash Design and Development for Devices*, and *Generator and Flash Demystified*.

Mike received his Masters in International Economics and European Studies from the John Hopkins School of Advanced International Studies (SAIS) in 1998.

When he is not programming, Mike can be found playing Halo, trying to recover from his World of Warcraft addiction, or hanging out with his two daughters, Isabel and Aubrey and wife Cathy.

Mike maintains a weblog at *http://www.mikechambers.com/blog/*.

Daniel Dura

Currently based in San Francisco, California, Daniel Dura is a Platform Evangelist at Adobe focusing on Apollo and Flash. Before joining Macromedia (which merged with Adobe in 2005), Daniel and his brother Josh founded Dura Media LLC, a rich Internet application development company based in Dallas, Texas. While at Adobe, he was a member of the Central and Flex teams, as well as a Product Manager for Developer Relations.

Daniel has given presentations on Flash, Apollo, and Flex all over the world at user group meetings, conferences, and pretty much anywhere someone is willing to listen. Outside of his day job, he enjoys general aviation and is well on his way to earning his private pilot license.

Kevin Hoyt

Kevin Hoyt is a Platform Evangelist with Adobe Systems, Inc. who likes moving, breaking, blurring and jumping over the lines of conventional technology. He seeks out every opportunity to congregate with other like-minded developers, and explore ways to escape any lines that form a box. Pushing the envelope of what technology can do, and how people perceive and interact with it, is his passion.

A frequent traveler, Kevin can generally be found deep in code while speaking with customers, at conferences, in front of user groups, or anywhere else they will give him time in front of an audience. The rest of the time he enjoys spending with his family at home in Parker, CO and indulging his photography habit.

This current chapter in Kevin's career started when he accepted a job with Allaire Corporation, circa 2000, with focus on ColdFusion and JRun. Allaire was purchased by Macromedia, Inc. in 2001, where he was able to unleash the latent designer within and help promote the value of rich Internet applications. Adobe acquired Macromedia in 2005, and Kevin now finds himself helping the company and its customers make sense of the increasingly large stable of products.

Acknowledgments

The authors would like to thank Mark Nichoson from Adobe and Steve Weiss, Philip Dangler, and Michele Filshie from O'Reilly for helping make the book possible in an incredibly short amount of time. We would also like to thank Adrian Ludwig, Laurel Reitman, Chris Brichford, Lucas Adamski, Rob Dixon and Jeff Swartz, all from Adobe, for input and work on the book.

Thank you to everyone on the AIR team for all of the dedication and hard work in getting a 1.0 runtime out the door.

CHAPTER 1

Introduction to the Adobe Integrated Runtime (AIR)

The Adobe Integrated Runtime (AIR) is a cross-platform desktop runtime being developed by Adobe that allows web developers to use web technologies to build and deploy Rich Internet Applications and web applications to the desktop.

TIP

Prior to the public beta release, the Adobe Integrated Runtime (AIR) was referred to in public by its code name of Apollo.

In order to better understand what Adobe AIR enables, and which problems it tries to address, it is useful to first take a look at the (relatively short) history of web applications.

A Short History of Web Applications

Over the past couple of years, there has been an accelerating trend of applications moving from the desktop to the web browser. This has been driven by a number of factors, which include:

- Growth of the Internet as a communication medium
- Relative ease of deployment of web applications
- Ability to target multiple operating systems via the browser
- Maturity of higher-level client technologies, such as the browser and the Flash Player runtime

Early web applications were built primarily with HTML and JavaScript, which, for the most part, relied heavily on client/server interactions and page refreshes. This page refresh model was consistent with the document-based metaphor for which the browser was originally designed, but provided a relatively poor user experience when displaying applications.

With the maturation of the Flash Player runtime, however, and more recently Ajax-type functionality in the browser, it became possible for developers to begin breaking away from page-based application flows. Developers began to be able to offer richer application experiences via the browser. In a whitepaper from March 2002, Macromedia coined the term rich Internet application (RIA), to describe these new types of applications in browsers, which "blend content, application logic and communications...to make the Internet more usable and enjoyable." These applications provided richer, more desktop-like experiences, while still retaining the core cross-platform nature of the Web:

> Internet applications are all about reach. The promise of the web is one of content and applications anywhere, regardless of the platform or device. Rich clients must embrace and support all popular desktop operating systems, as well as the broadest range of emerging device platforms such as smart phones, PDAs, set-top boxes, game consoles, and Internet appliances.

TIP

You can find the complete whitepaper and more information on RIAs at: *http://download.macromedia.com/pub/flash/whitepapers/richclient.pdf*

The paper goes on to list some features that define RIAs:

- Provide an efficient, high-performance runtime for executing code, content, and communications.
- Integrate content, communications, and application interfaces into a common environment.

- Provide powerful and extensible object models for interactivity.
- Enable rapid application development through components and reuse.
- Enable the use of web and data services provided by application servers.
- Embrace connected and disconnected clients.
- Enable easy deployment on multiple platforms and devices.

This movement toward providing richer, more desktop-like application experiences in the browser (enabled by the Flash Player runtime, and more recently by Ajax) has led to an explosion of web applications.

Today the web has firmly established itself as an application deployment platform that offers benefits to both developers and end users. Some of these benefits include the ability to:

- Target multiple platforms and operating systems.
- Develop with relatively high-level programming and layout languages.
- Allow end users to access their applications and data from virtually any Internet-connected computer.
- Easily push application updates to users.

The growth of web applications can be seen in both the Web 2.0 movement, which consists almost entirely of web based applications and APIs, as well as the adoption of web applications as a core business model by major companies and organizations.

Problems with Delivering Applications via the Browser

As web applications have become more complex, they have begun to push the boundaries of both the capabilities of the browser and the usability of the application. As their popularity grows, these issues become more apparent and important and highlight the fact that there are still a number of significant issues for both developers and end users when deploying and using applications within the browser.

The web browser was originally designed to deliver and display HTML-based documents. Indeed, the basic design of the browser has not significantly shifted from this purpose. This fundamental conflict between document- and application-focused functionality creates a number of problems when deploying applications via the browser.

Conflicting UI

Applications deployed via the browser have their own user interface, which often conflicts with the user interface of the browser. This application within an application model often results in user interfaces that conflict with and contradict each other. This can lead to user confusion in the best cases, and application failure in the worst cases. The classic example of this is the browser's Back button. The Back button makes sense when browsing documents, but it does not always make sense in the context of an application. Although there are a number of solutions that attempt to solve this problem, they are applied to applications inconsistently and users may not know whether a specific application supports the Back button, or whether it will force their application to unload, causing it to lose its state and data.

Distance from the Desktop

Due in part to the web security model (which restricts access to the user's machine), applications that run in the browser often do not support the type of user interactions with the operating system that people expect from applications. For example, you cannot drag a file into a browser-based application and have the application act on that file. Nor can the web application interact with other applications on the user's computer.

RIAs have tried to improve on this by making richer, more desktop-like interfaces possible in the browser, but they have not been able to overcome the fundamental limitations and separation of the browser from the desktop.

Primarily Online Experience

Because web applications are delivered from a server and do not reside on the user's machine, web applications are a primarily online experience. While there are attempts underway to make offline web-based applications possible, they do not provide a consistent development model and they fail to work across different browsers or require additional extensions to the browser to be installed by the user. In addition, they often require the user to interact with and manage their application and browser in complex and unexpected ways.

Lowest Common Denominator

Finally, as applications become richer and more complex and begin to push the boundaries of JavaScript and DHTML, developers are increasingly faced with differences in browser functionality and API implementations. While these issues can often be overcome with browser-specific code, they lead to code that's more difficult to maintain and scale, and takes time away from function-driven development of feature functionality.

While JavaScript frameworks are a popular way to help address these issues, they can offer only the functionality provided by the browser, and often resort to the lowest common denominator of features between browsers to ease the development model. The end result for JavaScript- or DHTML-based applications is a lowest common denominator user experience and interaction model, as well as increased development, testing, and deployment costs for the developer.

The fact that web applications have flourished despite these drawbacks is a testament to the attractiveness of having a platform with a good development model that has the ability to deliver applications to multiple operating systems. A platform that offered the reach and development model of the browser, while providing the functionality and richness of a desktop application, would provide the best of both worlds. This is what the Adobe Integrated Runtime aims to provide.

Introducing the Adobe Integrated Runtime

So, what is Adobe AIR, and how can it make web application development and deployment better?

The Adobe Integrated Runtime (AIR) is a cross-operating system runtime being developed by Adobe that allows web developers to leverage their existing web development skills (such as Flash, Flex, HTML, JavaScript, and PDF) to build and deploy rich Internet applications and content to the desktop.

In essence, Adobe AIR provides a platform in between the desktop and the browser, which combines the reach and ease of development of the web model with the functionality and richness of the desktop model.

It is important to step back for a second and point out what Adobe AIR is not. Adobe AIR is not a general desktop runtime meant to compete with lower-level application runtimes. Adobe AIR is coming from the web to the desktop and is targeted at web developers. Its primary use case is enabling web applications and RIAs to be deployed to the desktop. This is a very important but subtle distinction, as enabling web applications and RIAs on the desktop is the primary use case driving the Adobe AIR 1.0 feature set.

At its core, AIR is built on top of web technologies, which allow web developers to develop for and deploy to the desktop using the same technologies and development models that they use today when deploying applications on the Web.

Primary AIR Technologies

There are three primary technologies included within Adobe AIR, which fall into two distinct categories: application technologies and document technologies.

Primary Application Technologies

Application technologies are technologies that can be used as the basis of an application within Adobe AIR. Adobe AIR contains two primary application technologies, HTML and Flash, both of which can be used on their own to build and deploy AIR applications.

HTML / JavaScript

The first core application technology within Adobe AIR is HTML and JavaScript. This is a full HTML-rendering engine, which includes support for:

- HTML
- JavaScript
- CSS

- XHTML
- Document Object Model (DOM)

Yes, you read that right. You don't have to use Flash to build Adobe AIR applications. You can build full-featured applications using just HTML and JavaScript. This usually surprises some developers who expect Adobe AIR to focus only on Flash. However, at its core, Adobe AIR is a runtime targeted at web developers using web technologies—and what's more of a web technology than HTML and JavaScript?

The HTML engine used within Adobe AIR is the open source WebKit engine. This is the engine behind a number of browsers, including KHTML on KDE and Safari on Mac OS X.

TIP

You can find more information on the WebKit open source project at *http://www.webkit.org*.

See Chapter 3, "Working with JavaScript and HTML within Adobe AIR", for a more in-depth discussion of WebKit within Adobe AIR.

Flash

The second core application technology that Adobe AIR is built on is the Flash Player. Specifically, Adobe AIR is built on top of Flash Player 9, which includes the ECMAScript-based ActionScript 3, as well as the open source Tamarin virtual machine (which will be used to interpret JavaScript in future versions of Firefox).

TIP

You can find more information on the open source Tamarin project at on the Mozilla web site at *http://www.mozilla.org/projects/tamarin/*.

Not only are all of the existing Flash Player APIs available within Adobe AIR, but some of those APIs have also been expanded and/or enhanced. Some of the functionality that the Flash Player provides to Adobe AIR includes:

- Just-in-time Interpreted ActionScript engine for speedy application performance
- Full networking stack, including HTTP and RTMP, as well as Binary and XML sockets
- Complete vector-based rendering engine and drawing APIs
- Extensive multimedia support including bitmaps, vectors, audio, and video

---

TIP

Flash Player and ActionScript APIs are available to JavaScript within Adobe AIR applications.

Of course, the Flex 2 RIA framework is built on top of ActionScript 3, which means that you can take advantage of all of the features and functionality that Flex offers in order to build Adobe AIR applications.

Primary Document Technologies

Document technologies within Adobe AIR refer to technologies that can be used for the rendering of and interaction with electronic documents.

PDF and HTML are the primary document technologies available within Adobe AIR.

PDF

The Portable Document Format (PDF) is the web standard for delivering and displaying electronic documents on the Web.

PDF functionality requires that Adobe Reader version 8.1. be installed on the user's computer. If Adobe Reader 8.1 is installed, then Adobe AIR applications will be able to take full advantage of all of the features that reader also exposes when running within a web browser.

HTML

HTML was originally designed as a document technology, and today it provides rich and robust control over content and text layout and styling. HTML can be used as a document technology within Adobe AIR—both within an existing HTML application as well as within a Flash-based application.

What Does an Adobe AIR Application Contain?

Now that we know what technologies are available to applications running on top of the Adobe Integrated Runtime (see Figure 1-1), let's look at how those technologies can be combined to build an Adobe AIR application.

Applications can consist of the following combinations of technologies:

- HTML/JavaScript only
- HTML/JavaScript-based with Flash content
- Flash only (including Flex)
- Flash-based with HTML content
- All combinations can leverage PDF content

TIP

Flash content within HTML is not implemented in the public beta of Adobe AIR, although it will be available in the 1.0 release.

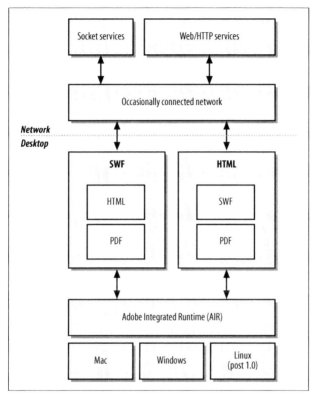

Figure 1-1. Adobe AIR application structure

Technology Integration and Script Bridging

Because WebKit and the Flash Player are both included within the runtime, they are integrated together on a very low level. For example, when HTML is included within Flash content, it's actually rendered via the Flash display pipeline, which, among other things, means that anything that you can do to a bitmap within Flash (blur, rotate, transform, etc.) you can also do to HTML.

This low-level integration also applies to the script engines within Adobe AIR that run ActionScript and JavaScript. Adobe AIR provides script bridging between the two languages and environments, which makes the following possible:

- JavaScript code can call AIR, Flash Player and Action-Script APIs
- ActionScript code can call JavaScript APIs
- ActionScript code can directly manipulate the HTML DOM
- Event registration both ways between JavaScript and ActionScript

Note that the script bridging is "pass by reference." So when passing an object instance from JavaScript to ActionScript (or vice versa), changes to that instance in one environment will affect the instance in the other environment. Among other things, this makes it possible to instantiate and use Flash Player APIs directly from JavaScript, or to register and listen for events.

This low-level script bridging between the two environments makes it very easy for developers to create applications that are a combination of both HTML and Flash.

TIP

Accessing ActionScript and Adobe AIR APIs from JavaScript is covered in more detail in Chapter 3.

The end result of all of this is that if you are a web developer using HTML and JavaScript, then you already have all of the skills necessary to build an Adobe AIR application.

Adobe AIR Functionality

If Adobe AIR did not provide additional functionality and APIs and simply allowed web applications to run on the desktop, it would not be quite as compelling. Fortunately, Adobe AIR provides a rich set of programming APIs, as well as close integration with the desktop that allows developers to build applications that take advantage of the fact that they're running on the user's desktop.

Adobe AIR Programming APIs

In addition to all of the functionality and APIs already offered by the Flash Player and WebKit engine, Adobe AIR provides additional functionality and APIs.

TIP

Adobe AIR APIs are available to both ActionScript and JavaScript.

Some of the new functionality includes, but is not limited to:

- Complete file I/O API
- Complete native windowing API
- Complete native menuing API (Mac only in beta)
- Online/Offline APIs to detect when service connectivity has changed
- Complete control over application chrome
- Local storage/settings APIs
- System notification APIs that tie into OS-specific notification mechanisms (not implemented in Beta)
- Application update APIs
- SQLite embedded database

Note that functionality may be implemented directly within the Adobe Integrated Runtime or on the framework layer (in Flex and JavaScript), or by using a combination of both.

Adobe AIR Desktop Integration

As discussed earlier, applications deployed via the browser cannot always support the same user interactions as desktop applications. This leads to applications that can be cumbersome for the user to interact with, as they do not allow the type of application interactions with which users are familiar.

Because an Adobe AIR application is a desktop application, it's able to provide the type of application interactions and experience that users expect from an application. This functionality includes, but is not limited to:

- Appropriate install/uninstall rituals
- Desktop install touch-points (such as shortcuts)
- Rich drag-and-drop support:
    —Between operating system and Adobe AIR applications
    —Between Adobe AIR applications
    —Between native applications and Adobe AIR applications
- Rich clipboard support
- System notifications
- Native icons

Once installed, an Adobe AIR application is just another native application, which means that the operating system and users can interact with it in the same as any other application. For example, things such as OS-level application prefetching and application switching work the same with Adobe AIR applications as they do with native applications.

The goal is that the end user does not need to know they are running an Adobe AIR application in order to be able to use it. They should be able to interact with an Adobe AIR application in the same way that they interact with any other application running on the desktop.

Security

All of this talk of APIs and desktop functionality brings up an important question: what about security? Because Adobe AIR applications have access to local resources, couldn't they theoretically do something harmful?

First, it is important to note that Adobe AIR runs on top of the operating system's security layer. It does not provide any way to get around or subvert this security. This is important, because it means Adobe AIR applications can work only within the permissions given to it by the operating system—and all current and any new security capabilities that the OS implements.

In order to run an Adobe AIR application, a user must download the application to the desktop, go through an install ritual, and then launch the application. This is an experience very similar to downloading and installing a desktop application. The similarity is not an accident. Adobe AIR applications run in a fundamentally different security content than applications that run within a browser. It is a security context closer to that of a native application than a web application.

To enable safe browsing, the browser security model limits all I/O capabilities of web applications. This includes restricting their ability to work with local resources, limiting what network resources are accessible, and constraining its user interface. The browser only allows applications to connect with data that is associated with (usually, provided by) a server located on a single web domain. In addition, the browser provides a trusted UI for users to understand the origin of the application and control the state of the application. This model is sufficient for applications that are connected to a single service provider and rely on that service for data synchronization and storage.

Some web developers have also stretched the browser security model by integrating data from multiple sources and/or by experimenting with user interfaces that are inconsistent with the browser chrome. Some of these applications require browser plug-ins with capabilities that aren't currently provided by the browsers. Others take advantage of browser features like user notification or customized security configurations to allow greater or lesser security to applications from specific domains. These mechanisms allow web developers to build more powerful applications, but they also are straining the browser security model.

Rather than trying to extend the web browser so that it can act as both a browser and as a flexible application runtime, Adobe AIR provides a flexible runtime for building applications using web technologies. Adobe AIR allows web developers to build applications that incorporate data from multiple sources, provide users with control over where and how their data is stored, and produce user experiences that are not possible within the browser's user interface. Because Adobe AIR applications must be installed on the desktop and require users to specifically trust the Adobe AIR application, Adobe AIR applications can safely exercise these capabilities. Browser-based applications cannot be granted these capabilities if the browser is to continue to fulfill its role as an application for safely browsing any web site on the Internet.

The Adobe AIR security model has a number of implications for application developers and users. For application developers, it means that content within an installed AIR application has capabilities that should not be exposed to any untrusted content, including files from the Web. The runtime has a number of features that are designed to reinforce that distinction and to help developers build applications using security best practices.

This also means that users should not install Adobe AIR applications from sources they do not trust. This is very similar to current practices for native desktop applications and for browser plug-ins. Many applications and web content require that browser plug-ins (such as Flash Player or Apple Quicktime) be installed in order to work. The Firefox browser has a very accessible extensibility layer that essentially allows any developer to extend the browser. These applications, plug-ins, and extensions can do potentially harmful things and therefore require that the user trust the source of the content.

Finally, one of the capabilities that will be included in the Adobe AIR 1.0 release is the ability of the runtime to verify the identity of an application's publisher. Users should carefully consider whether they want to trust the publisher of an application, as well as whether they want to install an application that hasn't been signed.

Adobe AIR Development Toolset

One of the reasons web applications have been successful is that they allow developers to easily deploy applications that users can run regardless of which OS they are on. Whether on Mac, Windows, Linux, Solaris, or cell phones, web applications provide reach.

However, success is based not only on cross-platform deployment, but also on the cross-platform nature of the development environment. This ensures that any developer can develop for—and leverage—the technology. Neither the runtime nor the development tools are tied to a specific OS.

The same is true of the Adobe Integrated Runtime. Not only does Adobe AIR provide the cross-platform reach of web applications, but, just as importantly, Adobe AIR applications can be developed and packaged on virtually any operating system.

Because Adobe AIR applications are built with existing web technologies such as HTML and Flash, you can use the same tools that you use to create browser-based content to create Adobe AIR applications. The Adobe AIR SDK provides a number of free command-line tools that make it possible to test, debug, and package Adobe AIR applications with virtually any web development and design tool.

ADL   Allows Adobe AIR applications to be run without having to first install them

ADT   Packages Adobe AIR applications into distributable installation packages

While Adobe will add support to its own web development and design tools for authoring Adobe AIR content, Adobe programs are not required to create applications. Using the Adobe AIR command-line tools, you can create an AIR application with any web development tool. You can use the same web development and design tools that you are already using today.

TIP

The Development Workflow will be covered in depth in Chapter 2.

Is Adobe AIR the End of Web Applications in the Browser?

So, by this point, you may be saying to yourself, "Gee, Adobe AIR sure sounds great! Why would anyone ever want to deploy an application to the browser again? Is Adobe AIR the end of web applications within the browser?"

No.

Let's repeat that again. No.

Adobe AIR solves most of the problems with deploying web applications via the browser. However, there are still advantages to deploying applications via the browser. The fact that there are so many web applications despite the disadvantages discussed earlier is a testament to the advantages of running within the browser. When those advantages outweigh the disadvantages, developers will still deploy their applications via the web browser.

But it's not necessarily an either/or question. Because Adobe AIR applications are built using web technologies, the application that you deploy via the web browser can be quickly turned into an Adobe AIR application. You can have a web-based version that provides the browser-based functionality, and then also have an AIR-based version that takes advantage of running on the desktop. Both versions could leverage the same technologies, languages, and code base. Indeed, some of the most popular early Adobe AIR applications, such as FineTune and eBay Desktop, complement existing web applications.

TIP

You can find more information on Finetune Desktop at *http://www.finetune.com/desktop/*.

You can find more information on eBay's "San Dimas" Adobe AIR application project at *http://blogs.ebay.com/projectsandimas*.

Adobe AIR applications complement web applications. They do not replace them.

CHAPTER 2

Getting Started with AIR Development

This chapter discusses how to get started developing applications for the Adobe Integrated Runtime using HTML and JavaScript. It covers:

- Installing Adobe AIR
- Configuring the Adobe AIR SDK and command-line tools
- Creating your first AIR application
- Testing AIR applications
- Packaging and deploying AIR applications

Once you have completed this chapter, your environment for developing AIR applications should be correctly configured, and you should have an solid understanding of how to begin to build, test, and deploy AIR applications.

What Do You Need to Develop AIR Applications?

There are a number of required items needed in order to begin developing AIR applications.

Adobe Integrated Runtime Beta

The AIR Beta is required to test application icons, as well as deployment of AIR applications. The Beta runtime can be downloaded for free from:

http://www.adobe.com/go/air

Adobe AIR SDK

The Adobe AIR SDK contains command-line tools, sample files, and other resources to make developing AIR applications easier. In particular, we will be using the command-line tools included in the SDK (ADL and ADT), which will allow us to test and package our AIR applications from virtually any development environment.

You can download the AIR SDK for free from:

http://www.adobe.com/go/air

HTML/JavaScript IDE or Editor

Building AIR applications with HTML and JavaScript requires that you have a way to create the HTML and JavaScript files. You can use any tool that supports creating and editing text files (such as VIM or Notepad), although it's recommended that you use a tool that has richer support for working with HTML and JavaScript files, such as Adobe Dreamweaver, Panic's Coda, or Aptana.

Supported Operating System

While it is possible to develop and package AIR applications on virtually any operating system (including Linux), you can test and deploy the application only on operating systems supported by Adobe AIR.

The supported operating systems for the Beta are:

- Windows XP SP2
- Windows Vista Home Ultimate Edition
- Mac OS 10.4.8 and 10.4.9 (Intel and PowerPC)

Adobe AIR will support additional versions of Mac and Windows for the 1.0 release, and Linux shortly after the 1.0 release.

Uninstalling Pre-Beta Versions of Adobe AIR

If you have previously installed an earlier version of Adobe AIR (formerly referred to as Apollo), you need to uninstall those versions before installing the Beta version.

Uninstalling on Windows

1. In the Windows Start menu, select Settings → Control Panel.
2. Select the Add or Remove Programs control panel.
3. Select Adobe Apollo 1.0 Alpha1 to uninstall the Apollo runtime.
4. Click the Change/Remove button.

Uninstalling on Mac

1. Delete the */Library/Frameworks/Adobe Apollo.framework* directory.
2. Delete the */Library/Receipts/Adobe Apollo.pkg* file.
3. Empty the Trash.

Once you have done this, you are ready to install the Beta runtime.

Installing Adobe AIR

While it is not necessary to have Adobe AIR installed on your computer in order to develop and test AIR applications, it is useful to have in order to try other AIR applications and to test your final application's deployment and packaging.

Installing the runtime is simple, and requires downloading and running the Adobe Integrated Runtime Installer.

1. Download AIR Installer from *http://www.adobe.com/go/air*
2. Launch the installer. On a Mac, you must first mount the *.dmg* file, which contains the installer.
3. Follow the installation instructions.

As Adobe AIR is simply a runtime and not an application that can be launched, the easiest way to confirm that it is installed correctly is to try installing an AIR application.

You can do this by either downloading an AIR application and installing it, or following the instructions later in the chapter to build a simple AIR application.

TIP

You can download sample AIR applications from Adobe's web site at: *http://www.adobe.com/go/air*.

Uninstalling Adobe AIR Beta

The process for uninstalling Adobe AIR is different depending on the operating system that you are running on.

Uninstalling on an Mac

The Adobe AIR installer places an uninstall application on the user's system when it is installed. To uninstall the Adobe Integrated Runtime, launch the uninstaller named *Adobe AIR Uninstaller* which can be found in the */Users/<User>/Applications* directory (where *<User>* is your system user account name).

Uninstalling on Windows

On Windows, you can uninstall Adobe AIR the same way that you uninstall any other application. Just select the Adobe Integrated Runtime in the add/remove programs section of the control panel.

Setting Up the AIR SDK and Command-Line Tools

The Adobe AIR SDK Beta contains tools, samples, and code that makes it easier to develop, test and deploy applications.

In particular, it contains two command-line tools that we will use:

ADL   This is used to launch and test an AIR application without having to first install it.

ADT   This is used to package an AIR application for distribution.

Installing the SDK

In order to ease development, you should place the path to these files within your system's path. This will allow you to execute the tools from anywhere on your system.

The command line tools are located in the bin directory within the SDK.

1. Download the AIR SDK Beta from *http://www.adobe.com/ go/air*.
2. Open the SDK
   a. On Windows, uncompress the ZIP archive.
   b. On Mac, mount the *.dmg* file.
3. Copy the contents of the SDK to your system (we will refer to this location as *<SDK_Path>*).

4. At this point, you should have at least the following two directories: *<SDK_Path>/bin* and *<SDK_Path>/runtime*. The ADL and ADT command-line tools are located in the bin directory.

Placing the Command-Line Tools Within the System Path

All that's left is to place the *<SDK_Path>/bin* directory into your system path, so that you can execute the command line applications from anywhere on your system.

The instructions for this are different depending on whether you are on a Mac- or Windows-based system.

Windows

1. Open the System Properties dialog box and click the Advanced tab. You can find this in the System settings in the Control Panel.
2. Click the Environment Variables button.
3. Select the PATH entry and then click the Edit button. Add the path to the *bin* directory to the end of the current variable value, separating it from previous values with a semicolon:

   ```
   ;<SDK_Path>/bin
   ```

   Figure 2-1 shows the process.
4. Click OK to close the panels.

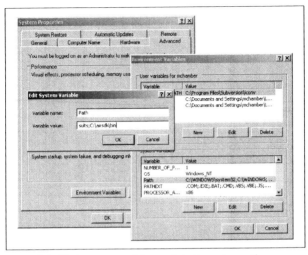

Figure 2-1. Placing command-line tools in the system path on Windows

In order to test the installation, open a new Windows Console (Start → Run → Console), and type:

```
adt
```

TIP

Make sure you open a new Console window; don't use a Console window that was already open.

You should see output similar this:

```
Too few arguments.
Usage: adt -package air_file app_xml [ file_or_dir |
 -C dir file_or_dir ... ] ...
```

This means that the tools are configured correctly.

If you get an error that the file cannot be found, then check the following things:

- Make sure that the *bin* and *runtime* directories are included in the <SDK_Path> *directory*
- Make sure that you included the path to <SDK_Path> directory correctly in the PATH environment variable.
- Make sure that you opened a new Console window before running the command.

Mac

There are a number of ways to add the path to the AIR SDK to your system path, depending on which shell you are using, and how you specify user environment variables.

The instructions below show how to modify your path environment variable if you are using the bash shell.

1. Open the Terminal program (*/Applications/Utilities/Terminal*)
2. Make sure you're in your home directory by typing **cd** and pressing enter.
3. We need to check to see if one of two files are present. Run the following command **ls -la**
4. Look for a file named either *.profile* or *.bashrc*.
5. If you have neither the *.profile* or *.bashrc* file, then create the *.profile* file with the following command:

        touch .profile

6. Open the *.profile* or *.bashrc* file with a text editor.
7. Look for a line that looks similar to this:

        export PATH=$PATH:/usr/local/bin

8. Add the path to the <SDK_Path>/*bin* directory to the end of this line. For example, if <SDK_Path>/*bin* is at */airsdk/bin*, the export path should look something like this:

        export PATH=$PATH:/usr/local/bin;/airsdk/bin

    making sure to separate the entries with a colon.

9. If the file is empty, add the following line:

```
export PATH=$PATH:/airsdk/bin
```

10. Save and close the file.

11. Run the following command to load the new settings source, *.profile* (or *.bashrc*, if that is the file you edited).

12. You can confirm that the new settings have taken effect by typing **echo $PATH** and pressing Enter. Make sure that the *<SDK_Path>/bin* path is included in the output.

13. In order to test the installation, open a Terminal window and type **adt**.

You should see output similar this:

```
Too few arguments.
Usage: adt -package air_file app_xml [ file_or_dir |
  -C dir file_or_dir ... ] ...
```

meaning that the tools are configured correctly.

If you get an error that the file cannot be found, then check the following things:

• Make sure the *bin* and *runtime* directories are included in the *<SDK_Path>* directory.

• Make sure you included the path to *<SDK_Path>/bin* correctly in the PATH environment variable.

• Make sure you either opened a new Terminal window, or ran *source* on your configuration file.

Creating a Simple AIR Application with HTML and JavaScript

Now that you have installed and configured Adobe AIR and the Adobe AIR SDK Betas, we are ready to build our first AIR application.

We will build a very simple "hello world" example. Once you have built and tested the application, your development environment will be set up and ready to build more complex and functional AIR applications.

Creating the Application Files

Every AIR application contains a minimum of two files. The first file is the root content file. This is the main HTML or SWF file for the application, and is the file that will be displayed/executed when the application first starts up.

The second file is called the application descriptor file, which is an XML file that provides metadata to Adobe AIR about the application.

Let's create these files for our application:

1. Create a new folder called *AIRHelloWorld*.
2. Inside of this folder, create two new files called *AIRHelloWorld.html* and *AIRHelloWorld.xml*.
3. Open each of these files using your favorite text or HTML editor/IDE.

Understanding application descriptor files

The application descriptor file is an XML file required for each AIR application. It provides general metadata (such as application name and description) to Adobe AIR, as well as information on how the application should be run. This includes specifying the root application file for the application and the window mode that the initial application window should use.

First, let's look at the entire application descriptor file (*AIRHelloWorld.xml*) for our application, and then we will go into more detail on each item within the file.

TIP

You can find a sample application descriptor file in the AIR SDK in the templates folder.

Open *AIRHelloWorld.xml* and type in the following text:

```xml
<?xml version="1.0" encoding="UTF-8"?>
<application xmlns="http://ns.adobe.com/air/application/1.0.M4"
                     appId="com.oreilly.AIRHelloWorld"
                     version="1.0">

    <name>AIRHelloWorld</name>
    <title>AIRHelloWorld Installer</title>
    <description>Simple Hello World Example
      using HTML</description>
     <copyright></copyright>

     <rootContent systemChrome="standard"
                  transparent="false" visible="true">
ApolloHelloWorld.html</rootContent>

</application>
```

The content should be pretty self-explanatory, but let's go through it line by line to understand what is going on.

```xml
<application xmlns="http://ns.adobe.com/air/application/1.0.M4"
                     appId="com.oreilly."
                     version="1.0">
```

There are two items worth pointing our here. First, the namespace definition:

```xml
xmlns="http://ns.adobe.com/air/application/1.0.M4"
```

This specifies the build of Adobe AIR that the application targets. In this case, it specifies 1.0.M4, which is the public Beta.

The `appId` property is important, and specifies a unique ID for the AIR application. Adobe AIR uses this ID to determine one application from another.

As you can see, it uses the reverse domain format, which you may be familiar with from some programming languages such as Java, ActionScript, and some JavaScript frameworks. You can create your own ID using your domain name and application name.

The next section of elements specify general metadata about the application:

```
<name>AIRHelloWorld</name>
<title>AIRHelloWorld Installer</title>
<description>Simple Hello World Example using HTML
</description>
<copyright></copyright>
```

Element	Description
name	The name of the application. This is the name that will be exposed to the operating system and user.
title	The title that will be used for the application installer.
description	A human readable description of the application that will be presented to the user during the installation process.
copyright	Optional. Allows the specification of Copyright information about the application.

The next element is the rootContent tag, which tells Adobe AIR which application file is the main root content of the application:

```
<rootContent systemChrome="standard"
              transparent="false" visible="true">
              ApolloHelloWorld.html</rootContent>
```

The value of the element should point to the main root file of the application, which, in this case, is an HTML file.

TIP

The application descriptor file and root content file must be in the same folder.

The rootContent element has a number of attributes that specify the initial window parameters and chrome of the application when it is first launched.

Element	Description
systemChrome	The type of systemChrome that the application should use ("standard" or "none").
transparent	Whether the application background should be transparent. If systemChrome is set to standard, this property is true.
visible	Whether the application is visible when it is first launched. This is useful if your application needs to perform some complex initialization before displaying the UI to the user.

For our example, we will use the operating system's window chrome.

This is all that is required for the application descriptor file for our application. At this point, we are ready to create the main HTML file for our application.

Creating the root application file

The root application file is the main file for the application that will be loaded when the application is launched. This file can be either a compiled Flash file (SWF) or an HTML file.

For this chapter, we will create a very simple HTML file in order to ensure that our development environment is configured correctly. We will cover more advanced AIR API usage in Chapters 3 and 4.

```
<html>
<head>
    <title>AIRHelloWorld</title>

    <script>
        function init()
        {
            runtime.trace("init function called");
        }
    </script>

</head>
<body onload="init()">
    <div align="center">Hello World</div>
</body>
</html>
```

As you can see, this is a very basic HTML file that displays "Hello World" and calls a JavaScript function once the file has loaded and initialized.

There are a couple of lines worth pointing out:

```
<body onload="init( )">
```

We just use the standard onload event on the body element to get an entry point for JavaScript into our application:

```
<script>
    function init( )
    {
        ...
    }
</script>
```

We then use a standard JavaScript function to capture the onload event.

Accessing AIR APIs

Looking at the init JavaScript function, you'll see some code you may not be familiar with:

```
runtime.trace("init function called");
```

This is the only AIR-specific code/markup in the entire application. The runtime property is a property placed on the window object by Adobe AIR which provides an entry point into the Adobe AIR engine and APIs. The trace function is a top-level AIR API which takes a string, and prints it out to the command line (when the application is launched via the command line).

All access to AIR-specific APIs (including Flash Player APIs) are accessed from JavaScript via the runtime property. We will cover this in more detail throughout the rest of the book.

Now that we have created both the application descriptor
file, as well as the root HTML application file, we are ready
to run and test our application within the runtime.

Testing the Application

While there are a number of HTML IDEs (such as
Dreamweaver) that are adding support for launching and
testing AIR applications directly from within the IDE, we will
focus on launching and testing AIR applications using the
ADL command-line tool included within the SDK. This will
provide a solid basis for an understanding of what is going
on. It will also provides the most flexibility in integrating the
development process with other IDEs, editors and work-
flows.

Using ADL to Launch the Application

The first step in testing the application is to run it as an AIR
application to make sure that:

- There are no errors in the application descriptor file
- The application launches
- The HTML renders correctly
- The JavaScript code functions as expected

While we could package up the entire application and then install it, this would be tedious, and make it difficult to quickly iterate on and test new versions. Luckily, the Adobe AIR SDK provides a command-line tool called ADL, which allows you to launch an AIR application without having to first install it.

In order to test our application:

1. Open a Terminal window (on Mac) or a Console window (on Windows).
2. Change to the directory that contains the *AIRHelloWorld.html* and *AIRHelloWorld.xml* files.
3. Run ADL with the following command, passing in the name of the application descriptor file:

   ```
   adl AIRHelloWorld.xml
   ```

This should launch your application within the standard system chrome of your operating system.

Figure 2-2. AIRHelloWorld application running from ADL on Mac OS X

If the application does not launch correctly, or if you get an error, check the following:

- Make sure you have configured the SDK correctly, so that the ADL tool can be found.
- Make sure that you are running the ADL command from the same directory that contains the *AIRHelloWorld.xml* file.
- Make sure that your application descriptor file contains well-formed XML.
- Make sure the information in the application descriptor file is correct. Pay particular attention to the application attributes and the `rootContent` value.
- Make sure that the `AIRHelloWorld.html` and `AIRHelloWorld.xml` files are in the same directory.

Once you have fixed any issues, and your application is running correctly, you can explore how to get information from the application at runtime.

Capturing Output from the Application at Runtime

When running applications from the command line via ADL, there are a number of ways to get runtime information and debugging information from the application.

Runtime JavaScript errors

Any runtime errors that arise from JavaScript execution while an AIR application launched via ADL is running will be output to ADL's standard out.

Let's modify our application to cause it to generate a JavaScript runtime error. Change the contents of *AIRHelloWorld.html* to:

```
<html>
<head>
    <title>AIRHelloWorld</title>

    <script>
```

```
        function init()
        {
            runtime2.trace("init function called");
        }
    </script>

</head>
<body onload="init()">
    <div align="center">Hello World</div>
</body>
</html>
```

All we did was change the init function to try and access a property named runtime2 that does not exist:

```
runtime2.trace("init function called");
```

Save the file, and run the application from ADL:

adl AIRHelloWorld.xml

The application should launch, and you should see the following error output from the command line that you launched the application from:

```
ReferenceError: Can't find variable: runtime2
init at app-resource:/AIRHelloWorld.html : 8
init at app-resource:/AIRHelloWorld.html : 8
onload at app-resource:/AIRHelloWorld.html : 13
```

This output provides the error, which in this case is that the variable named runtime2 cannot be found, as well as the line number that the error occurred on, and a stack trace of the execution call.

This information can be used to track down any errors within your application.

There are also times where the application may not be functioning correctly, but is not throwing any errors. In cases like this, it is useful to be able to capture information about the state of the application at runtime, in order to track down any issues.

Adobe AIR provides a function to make it possible to send information from the application to standard out at runtime.

runtime.trace

As we touched on earlier in the chapter, Adobe AIR provides a mechanism for sending Strings from JavaScript to the command line.

The trace function on the runtime property takes a string, which will then be output to ADL's standard out. Here is an example of its usage:

```
runtime.trace("This will be sent to standard out");
```

This can be useful for tracking information about the state of the application without having to interrupt the execution of the program.

Any non-String objects passed to trace will have their toString( ) function called. The JavaScript Object object provides a default toString( ) implementation, although some classes (such as Array) implement more context-sensitive toString( ) functions.

Here is an example of tracing an Array that contains various data types:

```
var a = ["a", 1, {foo:"bar"}];
runtime.trace(a);
```

This will result in the following output on the command line from ADL:

```
a,1,[object Object]
```

Of course, you can implement your own toString( ) method on your custom JavaScript classes, or override toString( ) functions on existing classes in order to provide more class-specific output.

Packaging and Deploying the AIR Application

Now that we understand how to build, test and debug an AIR application, we are ready to create an AIR file which will allow us to deploy and distribute our application.

What Is an AIR File?

An AIR file is a zip-based application distribution package that is used to distribute AIR applications. It contains all of the files necessary to install and run an AIR application, and is used by the Adobe Integrated Runtime to create and install an AIR application onto the user's system.

The AIR file is created by the ADT command line tool included in the AIR SDK and is used to distribute the application to other users.

TIP

AIR files require that Adobe AIR already be installed on the user's system.

ADL will be able to also create OS-specific native installers that will be able to first install Adobe AIR and then install the AIR application for systems where Adobe AIR is not already installed.

This functionality is not yet implemented in the public Beta.

An AIR file requires a minimum of two files, the application descriptor file, and a root application file. However, you can also include other files, icons, directories, and assets that will be bundled with the AIR file, and installed alongside your application. These files will then be available to the application at runtime.

Creating an AIR File Using ADT

The ADT command-line tool included in the Adobe AIR SDK is used to create AIR files. Its usage format is:

```
adl –package AIRFILENAME FILESTOINCLUDE
```

To create an AIR file for our application:

1. Open a terminal (Mac OS X) or Console (Windows) window.
2. Change to the directory which contains *AIRHelloWorld. html* and *AIRHelloWorld.xml*.
3. Run the following command:

```
adt -package AIRHelloWorld.air AIRHelloWorld.xml
AIRHelloWorld.html
```

This should create a file named *AIRHelloWorld.air* in the same directory. If the file is not created, or if you receive any errors:

- Make sure you have configured the SDK correctly in order to ensure that the ADT tool can be found.
- Make sure that you are running the ADT command from the same directory that contains the AIRHelloWorld.xml file.
- Make sure that your application descriptor file contains well formed XML.
- Make sure the information in the application descriptor file is correct. Pay particular attention to the application attributes, and the rootContent value.
- Make sure that the *AIRHelloWorld.html* and *AIRHelloWorld.xml* files are in the same directory

Testing the AIR File

Now that we have created the AIR file for our application, the only step left is to test the AIR file and make sure it installs correctly.

Testing the AIR file requires trying to install it onto the system, and then launching it:

1. Switch to the directory that contains the AIR file in Windows Explorer (Windows) or the Finder (Mac OS X).
2. Double-click the AIR file.
3. Follow the instructions in the install dialog box.
4. On the last screen of the install dialog box, make sure Run Application is checked.

You application should launch and run.

If it does not launch, or if you receive an error, check the following:

1. Make sure that you have correctly installed the Beta version of Adobe AIR.
2. Make sure that there were no errors when you created the AIR file via ADL.
3. Make sure that you have uninstalled any previous versions of Adobe AIR.

Once you have confirmed that the application is installed and runs correctly, you can relaunch it by clicking its icon. The default shortcut location varies, depending on your operating system:

System	Shortcut
Mac OS X	/Users/<USERNAME>/Applications
Windows	Start Menu → Programs → <APPLICATION NAME>

Deploying the AIR File

Once you have successfully created and packaged your AIR application, all that is left is to distribute the application. This is done by distributing the AIR file, either via the web, or directly via CD-ROM or other distribution mechanisms.

Setting the MIME type

One thing to watch out for when distributing AIR files for download from a web server, is to ensure that the MIME type is set correctly on the server. If the MIME type is not set correctly, web browsers may treat an AIR file as a zip file (and in the process rename it), or may display the raw bytes of the AIR file in the browser, instead of downloading it to the user's system.

The correct MIME type for an AIR file is:

```
application/vnd.adobe.air-application-installer-package+zip
```

For example, to set the MIME type for the Apache server, you would add the following line to your Apache configuration file:

```
AddType application/vnd.adobe.air-application-installer-
package+zip .air
```

Check the documentation for your web server for specific instruction on how to set the MIME type.

At this point, you have all of the basic knowledge of how to develop, test and deploy AIR applications, and are ready to begin to use the AIR APIs to build more full-featured and advanced applications.

CHAPTER 3

Working with JavaScript and HTML Within AIR

This chapter provides an in-depth overview of the HTML and JavaScript environments within the Adobe Integrated Runtime. It discusses:

- The use of the open source WebKit HTML-rendering engine within Adobe AIR
- JavaScript functionality within Adobe AIR
- AIR-specific implementations of functionality
- Working with AIR, Flash Player and ActionScript APIs from JavaScript

Once you have completed this chapter, you should have a solid understanding of the HTML and JavaScript environments within Adobe AIR. You should also understand how to work with AIR and ActionScript APIs within HTML and JavaScript-based applications.

WebKit Within the Adobe Integrated Runtime

Adobe AIR leverages the open source WebKit-rendering engine to add support for rendering HTML content to the runtime.

In addition to HTML rendering, WebKit also provides support for associated web technologies, such as:

- JavaScript
- XMLHttpRequest

- CSS
- XHTML
- W3C DOM Level 2 support

Essentially, Adobe AIR has a full HTML rendering engine, and includes support for of the same technologies that can be used when developing web applications and content targeting the web browser. Developers can build full-featured AIR applications that leverage these technologies.

TIP

You can find more information on the WebKit project at: *http://www.webkit.org.*

Why WebKit?

Adobe spent a considerable amount of time researching which HTML engine to use within Adobe AIR and used a number of criteria that ultimately led them to settle on WebKit.

Open project

Adobe knew from the very beginning that it did not want to create and maintain its own HTML rendering engine. Not only would this be an immense amount of work, but it would also make it difficult for developers, who would then have to become familiar with all of the quirks of yet another HTML engine.

WebKit provides Adobe AIR with a full-featured HTML engine that is under continuous development by a robust development community that includes individual developers as well as large companies such as Nokia and Apple. This allows Adobe to focus on bug fixes and features, and also means that Adobe can actively contribute back to WebKit, while also taking advantage of the contributions made by other members of the WebKit project.

Proven technology that web developers know

As discussed earlier, one of the biggest problems with complex web application development is ensuring that content works consistently across browsers. While something may work perfectly in Firefox on the Mac, it may completely fail in Internet Explorer on Windows. Because of this, testing and debugging browser-based content can be a nightmare for developers.

Adobe wanted to ensure that developers were already familiar with the HTML engine used within Adobe AIR, so they did not have to learn all of the quirks and bugs of a new engine. Since Safari (which is built on top of WebKit) is the default browser for Mac OS X (and is also available on Windows), developers should be familiar with developing for WebKit.

Minimum effect on AIR runtime size

The target size for Adobe AIR is between 5 and 9 MB. The WebKit code base was well-written and organized and has had a minimal impact on the final AIR runtime.

Proven ability to run on mobile devices

While the first release of Adobe AIR runs only on personal computers, the long-term vision is to extend Adobe AIR from the desktop to cell phones and other devices. WebKit has a proven ability to run on such devices and has been ported to cell phones by both Nokia and Apple.

JavaScript Within AIR

Adobe AIR has full support for JavaScript within HTML content. JavaScript 1.5, which corresponds to ECMA-262 is supported.

The JavaScript engine is implemented via WebKit, and works the same as it does within WebKit-based browsers. In addition to having access to the HTML DOM, JavaScript can also access AIR and Flash Player APIs directly via the `window.runtime` property. This will be discussed in more detail later.

TIP

For an in-depth introduction and discussion of JavaScript, check out *JavaScript: the Definitive Guide*: 5th Edition, published by O'Reilly:

   http://www.oreilly.com/catalog/jscript5/

AIR Implementation of Functionality

HTML and JavaScript functionality is consistent with that found in other WebKit-based projects and browsers, such as Apple's Safari browser. When exploring documentation on HTML engine / browser functionality, you can use references to the Safari browser as an indicator of the functionality available within the HTML environment within AIR.

However, because the HTML engine is running in a runtime, and not a browser, there are a few differences that are useful to understand before beginning development with HTML and JavaScript within Adobe AIR.

Cookies

The Adobe Integrated Runtime has full support for setting and getting cookies from HTML-based content. Cookie support is implemented via the operating system's networking stack. This means that AIR applications can share cookies set by any browser or application that also leverage the operating system stack.

For example. AIR applications can share cookies set through Internet Explorer on Windows, and Safari on Mac, as they both also use the operating system's cookie storage functionality. Firefox implements its own cookie storage and thus

---

cookies set within Firefox cannot be shared with AIR applications.

Windowing

Windows

You can create new windows via JavaScript just as you can within the browser.

```
myWindow = window.open("Window.html", "myWindow",
"height=400,width=400");
```

However, the runtime property which provides access to AIR and Flash Player APIs is not automatically available within the new window. In order to make it available, you must explicitly place it within the scope of the new window like so:

```
window.runtime = window.opener.runtime;
```

Dialogs

HTML dialogs are also supported within AIR applications, although not all have been implemented within the Beta.

Dialog	Supported in Beta
alert	yes
confirm	yes
prompt	no

In addition, the file-browsing dialog created via:

```
<input type="file" />
```

is not currently supported within the Beta.

Any dialogs not currently supported in the Beta, will be supported in the 1.0 release.

XMLHttpRequest and Ajax

The XMLHttpRequest object, which enables the use of Ajax techniques for sending and loading data, is completely supported within AIR applications.

One advantage to developing Ajax applications within Adobe AIR versus the browser, is that because you have a consistent runtime to target across operating systems, you do not have to worry about cross-browser, platform inconsistencies in how the API is implemented.

The primary benefit of this is that you have to write only one version of the code.

Here's a simple example of an XMLHttpRequest object call within an AIR application that works regardless of which operating system the application is running on:

```
<script type="text/javascript">
    var xmlhttp;
    function appLoad()
    {
        //replace with URL to resource being loaded
        var url = "http://www.mikechambers.com/blog/";
        xmlhttp = new XMLHttpRequest();
        xmlhttp.open("GET", url,true);

        xmlhttp.onreadystatechange=function(){
            if (xmlhttp.readyState==4)
            {
                runtime.trace(xmlhttp.responseText);
            }
        }
```

```
            xmlhttp.send(null)
    }
  </script>
```

When called, this function uses the `XMLHttpRequest` object to load the specified URL and prints its contents out to the command line. The main thing to note in this example is that because the runtime is known and it is consistent across operating systems, you do not have to detect the existence of—or differences in—the implementation of `XMLHttpRequest` as you would when deploying in the browser.

Both synchronous and asynchronous `XMLHttpRequest` calls are supported, as is loading data across domains.

URI Schemes

Working with Universal Resource Identifiers (URIs) within HTML content in AIR applications is largely the same as working with URIs within the browser. This section gives a quick overview of working with URIs within HTML content in AIR applications, and introduces some new URIs made available by the runtime.

Supported URI schemes

Adobe AIR provides support for the most common URI schemes available within the browser (Table 3-1).

Table 3-1. Supported URI schemes

URI scheme	Description
http://	URI that points to a resource accessed via the standard HTTP protocol. This is fully supported within Adobe AIR.
https://	URI that points to a resource accessed via a protocol encrypted with SSL/TLS. This is fully supported within Adobe AIR.
file://	URI that points to a resource on the local or a networked file system.
ftp://	URI that points to a resource accessed with the FTP protocol. In the Adobe AIR Beta, requests for files will work correctly, while requests for directories return an empty page with no directory listing.

Unsupported URI schemes

In the Beta build of Adobe AIR, the commonly used *mailto://* and feed:// URI schemes are not available.

At the time that the book was written, it had not yet been determined whether and/or how these URI schemes would be available for the 1.0 release.

AIR URI Schemes

Adobe AIR provides a number of additional URIs that make it easy to reference files and content within specific areas of the users system (Table 3-2).

Table 3-2. Adobe AIR URI schemes

URI	Description
app-resource:/	Provides a reference to the root content directory of the application. This should be used when referencing content included within the AIR file.
app-storage:/	Provides a reference to an application-specific storage area on the user's system. This area is useful for storing user-specific application settings and content.

Here is a simple example of the app-resource AIR URI:

```
app-resource:/foo/test.html
```

This references a file name *test.html* in the *foo* directory that was installed with the application.

TIP

The AIR-specific URIs take only a single slash, versus two
slashes in the other URIs.

Within HTML content, these URI schemes can be used anywhere within HTML and JavaScript content where regular
HTTP URIs are used.

Relative URLs

You're not restricted to using just absolute URLs within AIR
applications. You can also use relative URLs, but it is important to remember that relative URLs within AIR applications
are relative to the application, and not to a server (as they
would be when doing traditional browser-based client/server
development).

Relative URLs will be relative to the root of the application,
and will resolve to the app-resource:/ URI.

For example:

```
<img src="foo/image.png" />
```

will resolve to:

```
<img src="app-resource:/foo/image.png" />
```

You should keep this in mind when moving web and
browser-based content and code into an AIR application.

Security

This section discusses a number of differences in the security
model implementations in the Adobe AIR, versus that in the
browser.

Security Context

Content installed within the application runs under the security context of the application. This means that it has access to all of the Adobe AIR APIs and functionality.

Remote content loaded into the application is run under a web security content, and as such does not have access to the Adobe AIR APIs and functionality, or to the expanded privileges to which application content has access.

For example, content loaded into the application via:

app-resource:/foo.html

has full access to the AIR APIs. However, content loaded using HTTP, like so:

http://www.yourdomain.com/foo.html

runs in a web security context, and does not have access to AIR APIs.

Content in the application install directory falls under the application security context. Content in the application storage directory (app-storage:/) falls under the web security context (Table 3-3).

Table 3-3. Application and web security contexts

URL data loaded from	Has access to AIR APIs?
app-resource:/foo.html	Yes
app-storage:/foo.html	No
http://www.anydomain.com/foo.html	No
https://www.anydomain.com/foo.html	No
file:/C:/foo.html	No
ftp://www.anydomain.com/foo.html	No

Because of this, content downloaded from third party sources and domains should always be placed in the *app-storage:/* directory, and not in the *app-resource:/* directory in order to prevent inadvertent elevation of security context and privileges.

Cross domain data loading

The Adobe Integrated Runtime does not enforce cross domain data loading restrictions for application content. Among other things, this allows the loading of data across domains using the XMLHttpRequest object.

Cross domain data loading restrictions are enforced for non-privileged web content.

Using JavaScript Frameworks

Because the HTML environment within the Adobe Integrated Runtime has full support for JavaScript, you can use virtually any JavaScript framework to build your application. However, when using frameworks, there are a couple of things to keep in mind:

- The framework should be included within your application's AIR file, in order to ensure that it is available offline.

- If the framework expects to load resources from a central server, you may have to test to make sure that relative URLs continue to work.

- While it is possible to load the framework from the network at runtime, this can lead to slower application startup performance, as well as an inability for the application to work when offline.

You can find a number of HTML-based AIR applications and their source built using the EXT-JS framework from the Adobe Labs AIR site at:

http://www.adobe.com/go/airwiki

TIP

You can find more information on the EXT-JS frame-work at http://extjs.com/.

Accessing AIR APIs from JavaScript

In addition to the standard JavaScript and HTML DOM APIs, JavaScript code running within the application context in an AIR application can also take advantage of APIs provided by the runtime, as well as Flash Player APIs and even ActionScript 3 libraries. This greatly extends the capabilities of JavaScript over the APIs available in the browser, and includes functionality such as:

* Playing sounds
* Manipulating images and bitmaps
* Reading and writing files to and from the local file system
* Creating, controlling and manipulating native windows
* Making direct socket connections (both binary and text based)
* Accessing the clipboard
* Leveraging an embedded database to store data

TIP

You can find examples of how to leverage these features in the cookbook section in Chapter 4.

This section discusses how to leverage AIR and Flash Player APIs from JavaScript, as well as how to load and leverage compiled ActionScript libraries from within JavaScript.

Accessing AIR and Flash Player APIs

Most AIR and Flash Player APIs are contained within packages (similar to how many JavaScript frameworks leverage namespaces and packages). This helps organize the APIs, and also reduces the possibility of naming conflicts. When accessing AIR and Flash Player APIs directly from JavaScript, you must do so via their complete package path and name.

As discussed earlier, all AIR and Flash Player APIs are made available via the `window.runtime` property. The runtime property is at the root of the runtime environment, and all APIs are relative to this root.

For example, to access an API which is not contained within a package, such as `trace( )` you reference it directly from the runtime property, like so:

```
window.runtime.trace("foo");
```

However, if you want to access an API that is contained within a package, you must prepend the package path to the API. For example, to access the amount of memory currently used by the application, you can call the `totalMemory` Flash Player property that is in the `flash.system.System` class. To call this API from JavaScript:

```
var mem = window.runtime.flash.system.System.totalMemory;
```

This also applies when creating new instances of an API class from within JavaScript:

```
var file = new window.runtime.flash.filesystem.File( );
```

This code creates a new `File` instance that can be used to work with the file system.

Here is a complete example that shows how to write a file named *output.txt* to the user's desktop:

```
//call a static property
var desktop = window.runtime.flash.filesystem.File.
desktopDirectory;
```

```
//call a function on an instance of a class
var file = desktop.resolve("output.txt");

//create a new instance of a class using new
var fileStream = new window.runtime.flash.filesystem.
FileStream( );

    //call a function, passing arguments
    fileStream.open(file, window.runtime.flash.filesystem.
              FileMode.WRITE);

    fileStream.writeUTFBytes("Hello World");
    fileStream.close( );
```

Don't worry too much about what the code is doing in this example, but rather focus on how the AIR APIs are called from JavaScript.

This allows you to leverage virtually any AIR or Flash Player API from within JavaScript.

TIP

Download JavaScript specific language references for AIR from the Adobe web site at: *http://www.adobe.com/go/air*.

By remembering how to use the package structure to call APIs, you can leverage all AIR, Flash Player and ActionScript APIs even if JavaScript-specific documentation is not provided.

Working with AIR and Flash Player Events

Many of the AIR and Flash Player APIs make extensive use of events. Event handling in ActionScript-based APIs is based on the W3C DOM Level 3 event model. This is similar to the W3C DOM Level 2 event model available within JavaScript, but is very different from the callback mechanism often deployed in JavaScript.

In order to be notified when an event from an AIR or Flash Player API occurs, you must register to listen for it. The best

---

way to understand this is to look at an example. The following example registers for a NETWORK_CHANGE event that is broadcast by the Shell class:

```
function onNetworkChange(event)
{
    runtime.trace("Network status changed");
}

function onAppLoad( )
{
    window.runtime.flash.system.Shell.shell.addEventListener(
            window.runtime.flash.events.Event.NETWORK_CHANGE,
            onNetworkChange);
}
```

As you can see from the example, you register for events broadcast by a class instance by calling the addEventListener function on the class instance. This API requires two arguments.

The first argument is the event name of the event being broadcast. For all AIR and Flash Player APIs, there will be a constant for the event name, which you can find in the documentation.

The second argument is a reference to the function that will handle the event. In this case, the function is named onNetworkChange. Looking at the function, you can see that it is passed an argument with information about the event. Again, all AIR and Flash Player APIs will pass an object to the event handler function, which provides information about the event. You can find the exact type of event object passed to the handler, and the information it provides, by referencing the API documentation.

Using AIRAliases.js

As the previous examples show, being able to leverage AIR and Flash Player APIs from directly within JavaScript can be very powerful. However, because you must reference the

APIs via the runtime property and the complete API package path, it can lead to very verbose code.

In order to make it easier to use some of the more common AIR and Flash Player APIs from within JavaScript, Adobe has created a JavaScript include file, named *AIRAliases.js*. This file, which can be found in the *frameworks* directory of the SDK, provides aliases for commonly used APIs to make them more convenient to use from within JavaScript.

To use the aliases file, copy it from the SDK to your application directory (make sure to also package it in your AIR file). You then include it within your application using the script tag in each HTML document that you want to leverage the aliases in.

For example, let's look at the earlier example that writes a file to the desktop, but uses the JavaScript aliases provided in the *AIRAliases.js* file instead of typing out the complete package paths:

```
<script src="AIRAliases.js"></script>

<script type="text/javascript">
    function writeFile()
    {
        var desktop = air.File.desktopDirectory;
        var file = desktop.resolve("output.txt");
        var fileStream = new air.FileStream();
            fileStream.open(file, air.FileMode.WRITE);
            fileStream.writeUTFBytes("Hello World");
            fileStream.close();
    }
</script>
```

First, notice that the code is much less verbose. This is because instead of having to reference APIs via `window.runtime` and then their complete package path, we can use the aliases within the include file.

For example, this reduces:

```
var desktop = window.runtime.flash.filesystem.File.
desktopDirectory;
```

to:

```
var desktop = air.File.desktopDirectory;
```

Second, the AIR and Flash Player APIs are placed in a namespace called air. If you open the *AIRAliases.js* file, you can see how the aliases actually work. For example, here is the code that sets up the File API aliases:

```
var air; if (!air) air = {};

// file
air.File = window.runtime.flash.filesystem.File;
air.FileStream = window.runtime.flash.filesystem.
FileStream;
air.FileMode = window.runtime.flash.filesystem.FileMode;
```

To see a complete list of APIs included, open up the *AIRAliases.js* file with a text editor. While not all APIs are included, you can easily add additional APIs by following the existing examples in the file.

Leveraging Compiled ActionScript Libraries

Not only can AIR applications leverage Flash Player APIs directly from JavaScript, they can also access compiled ActionScript 3 libraries from within JavaScript.

In addition to loading external JavaScript files, the HTML script tag within an AIR application also has support for loading compiled ActionScript 3 libraries and providing access to the ActionScript classes included within the file. Once the SWF is loaded, the APIs can be referenced in the same manner as the AIR and Flash Player APIs are referenced via the API package path and API name.

Let's look at an example. Included in the Adobe AIR SDK is a SWF that contains the ActionScript 3 Adobe AIR service connectivity API. While this example won't show how to use that API, it will show how to access those APIs from within JavaScript.

In order for the example to work, you must copy the *frameworks/servicemonitor.swf* file from the AIR SDK to your application directory.

Any classes and APIs available within the compiled SWF will be made available via the `window.runtime` property. The API we want to reference is in a class named `ServiceMonitor` in the `air.net` package.

Here's the code:

```
<script src="servicemonitor.swf"></script>

<script>
    function onAppLoad( )
    {
        var monitor = new runtime.air.net.ServiceMonitor();
    }
</script>
```

This is a very simple example that shows how to load compiled ActionScript libraries, and then access them from JavaScript. In this case, we include the *servicemonitor.swf* file via the HTML script tag. This file contains the compiled Action-Script 3 APIs for the `air.net.ServiceMonitor` class.

Using this technique allows you to leverage third party ActionScript APIs from within AIR applications via JavaScript.

At this point, you should have a good understanding of the HTML and JavaScript environments within the Adobe Integrated Runtime, as well as how to leverage AIR, Flash Player and third-party ActionScript 3 APIs directly from JavaScript. The rest of the book will use this knowledge to show how to accomplish specific tasks from HTML and JavaScript applications running within Adobe AIR.

CHAPTER 4

AIR Mini-Cookbook

This chapter describes solutions to common tasks when developing AIR applications. The solutions in this chapter illustrate many concepts used in AIR application development, and provide working HTML and JavaScript code that can be leveraged within your application.

NOTE

All examples in this chapter assume you are using the *AIRAliases.js* file.

Application Chrome

Adding Custom Controls

Problem

You want to create custom window chrome for your application and need the ability for the user to close and minimize the application.

Solution

Use native window APIs within Adobe AIR to hook up, minimize, and close button functionality.

Discussion

While Adobe AIR allows developers to completely define and customize the application's window chrome, it is important to remember that the application is responsible for every type of windowing event that might normally occur. This means connecting the various visual elements with their respective operating system events.

The `NativeWindow` instance that represents the main application window is not directly accessible from inside the main HTML DOM. Using AIR APIs, an application can traverse outside of the HTML control, out to the `Stage`, and get a reference to its `NativeWindow` instance. Once a reference to the native window has been obtained, the appropriate methods can be called to trigger the operating-system specific event (or vice versa). In the case of being able to minimize the window, the application can use `NativeWindow.minimize()` and `NativeWindow.close()` in the case of closing:

```
window.htmlControl.stage.window.minimize();
window.htmlControl.stage.window.close();
```

The `NativeWindow.close()` event does not necessarily terminate the application. If only one application window is available, the application will terminate. If there are multiple windows, they will close until only one window remains. Closing the last window terminates the application.

application.xml

```
<?xml version="1.0" encoding="utf-8" ?>
<application
    xmlns="http://ns.adobe.com/air/application/1.0.M4"
    appId="com.adobe.demo.html.CustomChrome"
    version="1.0 Beta">

    <name>Custom Chrome</name>
    <title>Custom Chrome</title>

<rootContent
    visible="true"
    transparent="true"
```

```
            systemChrome="none"
            width="206"
            height="206">

            custom.html

    </rootContent>

</application>
```

index.html

```html
<html>
<head>

<title>Custom Window Controls</title>

<style>
body {
    background-image: url( 'custom-chrome.gif' );
    font-family: Verdana, Geneva, Arial, Helvetica, sans-serif;
    font-size: 12px;
}

#closer {
    position: absolute;
    width: 70px;
    left: 68px;
    top: 105px;
}

#minimize {
    position: absolute;
    width: 70px;
    left: 68px;
    top: 75px;
}

textarea {
    position: absolute;
    left: 8px;
    right: 8px;
    bottom: 8px;
    top: 36px;
    border-color: #B3B3B3;
}
```

```
#title {
    position: absolute;
    font-weight: bold;
    color: #FFFFFF;
}
</style>

<script type="text/javascript" src="AIRAliases.js"></
script>

<script>
function doClose( )
{
    window.htmlControl.stage.window.close( );
}

function doLoad( )
{
    document.getElementById( "minimize" ).
addEventListener( "click", doMinimize );
document.getElementById( "closer" ).addEventListener(
"click", doClose );
}

function doMinimize( )
{
    window.htmlControl.stage.window.minimize( );
}
</script>

</head>
<body onload="doLoad( )">

<input id="minimize" type="button" value="Minimize" />
<input id="closer" type="button" value="Close" />

</body>
</html>
```

Windowing

Creating a New Window

Problem

You need to display an additional widow into which additional content can be loaded.

Solution

Basic windows can be generated and maintained in a similar fashion as traditional HTML content using the `window.open( )` method.

Discussion

The JavaScript `window.open( )` method invokes a new window similar to the way it would when used in the browser. Content that gets loaded into the new window can come from a local file, or URL endpoint. Similar to windows created using JavaScript in the browser, there is finite control over the window itself. The window properties that can be controlled are width, height, scrollbars, and resizable.

```
var login = window.open( "login.html", "login", "width =
300, height = 200" );
```

A native window is a better choice when additional control over the new window is required. Native windows expose virtually the entire functionality of the operating system such as minimize/maximize, always in front, full screen and even removal of system chrome altogether. The drawback to using native windows is that there is substantially more work because all events must be monitored and managed explicitly.

TIP

The `window.opener` property that is commonly used in JavaScript to refer from a new window to the parent (creating) window can also be used.

```
<html>
<head>

<title>Basic Window</title>
<script type="text/javascript" src="AIRAliases.js">
</script>

<script>
function doLoad()
{
    document.getElementById( "btnLogin" ).
addEventListener( "click", doLogin );
}

function doLogin()
{
    var login = window.open( "Login.html", null,
                             "width = 270, height = 150" );
}
</script>

</head>
<body onload="doLoad()">

<input id="btnLogin" type="button" value="Login" />

</body>
</html>

Login.html
<html>
<head>

<title>Login</title>

</head>
<body>

<table>
    <tr>
        <td>Email:</td>
        <td><input name="email" /></td>
    </tr>
    <tr>
        <td>Password:</td>
```

```
                <td><input name="password" /></td>
        </tr>
        <tr>
            <td colspan="2" align="right">
                <input type="button" value="Sign In" />
            </td>
        </tr>
    </table>

    </body>
    </html>
```

Creating a New Native Window

Problem

You need to display an additional window into which additional content can be loaded, and you need to be able to fine tune how the new window appears.

Solution

The `NativeWindow` class provides the foundation for creating and managing new windows that require a high degree of customization and control.

Discussion

Native windows make an excellent choice for creating and managing new windows that require a high degree of customization. You may want the application to hide the minimize/maximize buttons. You may also want to control window z-ordering, or force a particular window to always stay on top. The `NativeWindow` class offers control over these aspects of a window and more.

The `NativeWindow` constructor takes two arguments; a Boolean specifying whether or not the window is initially visible, and a `NativeWindowInitOptions` object which controls aspects of the window such as whether or not it is resizable, or even if it has any system chrome at all. The `NativeWindowInitOptions` constructor takes no arguments:

```
var options = new air.NativeWindowInitOptions( );
var login = null;

options.minimizable = false;
options.maximizable = false;
options.resizable = false;

login = new air.NativeWindow( false, options );
```

Not all the options an application may make use of appear as initialization options. Additional options that may be controlled on an instance of NativeWindow itself include the window title, whether or not it is always in front, and window sizing and positioning.

TIP

If you intend to manage the initial window size manually, it is best to start with an invisible window. Creating a native window and then changing its positioning and layout in the same block of code results in a quick flicker of the window as it is initially painted and then relocated and resized.

When using the NativeWindow class, you have absolute control over its appearance, behavior and content. If the window is to be resized, the operating system will merely provide for the handles and resizing operations. The size, position, content, and layout of the window itself must be controlled by the application. Depending on how the application needs to handle resizing, the NativeWindowBoundsEvent.RESIZE or NativeWindowBoundsEvent.RESIZING events may be used:

```
login.title = "Login";
login.alwaysInFront = false;
login.bounds = new window.runtime.flash.geom.Rectangle(
    ( air.Capabilities.screenResolutionX - 270 ) / 2,
    ( air.Capabilities.screenResolutionY - 150 ) / 2,
    270,
    150 );
login.visible = true;
```

A native window initially has no content outside of the runtime. Unlike the JavaScript window.open( ) method, an application cannot simply specify a URL for the content to be displayed. The window is so raw that an application must first add an HTMLControl to the window, size it, and tell it what content to load. The HTMLControl constructor takes no arguments, exposes properties for width and height, and exposes an HTMLControl.load( ) method which can be used to load external content:

```
var control = new window.runtime.flash.html.HTMLControl( );
var page =
air.File.applicationResourceDirectory.resolve( "login.html" );

control.width = login.stage.stageWidth;
control.height = login.stage.stageHeight;
control.load( new air.URLRequest( page.url ) );
```

The NativeWindow.stage property represents a Stage object and is used to determine the viewable area for sizing the HTMLControl. Using NativeWindow.width or NativeWindow.height for the HTMLControl sizing would have resulted in an HTMLControl as large as the window itself (including chrome). Stage.stageWidth and Stage.stageHeight will size the control to fit the viewable area.

The Stage is also where controls will get added for display (called the display list), and is responsible for how the content inside of it will be positioned and sized. For most applications this means setting Stage.scaleMode to StageScaleMode.NO_SCALE and Stage.align to StageAlign.TOP_LEFT. Calling Stage.addChild( ) will add the HTMLControl to the viewable area. Using this approach, it is possible to have multiple HTMLControl controls in one single window:

```
win.stage.scaleMode = window.runtime.flash.display.
StageScaleMode.NO_SCALE;
win.stage.align = window.runtime.flash.display.StageAlign.
TOP_LEFT;
win.stage.addChild( control );
```

```html
<html>
<head>

<title>Native Window</title>
<script type="text/javascript" src="AIRAliases.js"></
script>

<script>
var Rectangle = window.runtime.flash.geom.Rectangle;

var control = null;
var win = null;

function doLoad( )
{
    document.getElementById( "btnLogin" ).
addEventListener( "click", doLogin );
}

function doLogin( )
{
    var options = new air.NativeWindowInitOptions( );
    var login = air.File.applicationResourceDirectory.
resolve( "login.html" );

    options.minimizable = false;
    options.maximizable = false;
    options.resizable = false;

    win = new air.NativeWindow( false, options );
    win.title = "Login";
    win.alwaysInFront = true;
    win.bounds = new Rectangle(
        ( air.Capabilities.screenResolutionX - 270 ) / 2,
        ( air.Capabilities.screenResolutionY - 150 ) / 2,
        270,
        150 );
    win.visible = true;
```

```
    control = new window.runtime.flash.html.HTMLControl( );
    control.width = win.stage.stageWidth;
    control.height = win.stage.stageHeight;
    control.load( new air.URLRequest( login.url ) );

    win.stage.scaleMode = window.runtime.flash.display.
StageScaleMode.NO_SCALE;
    win.stage.align = window.runtime.flash.display.
StageAlign.TOP_LEFT;
    win.stage.addChild( control );
}
</script>

</head>
<body onload="doLoad( )">

<input id="btnLogin" type="button" value="Login" />

</body>
</html>
```

Login.html

```
<html>
<head>

<title>Login</title>

</head>
<body>

<table>
    <tr>
        <td>Email:</td>
        <td><input name="email" /></td>
    </tr>
    <tr>
        <td>Password:</td>
        <td><input name="password" /></td>
    </tr>
```

```
    <tr>
        <td colspan="2" align="right">
            <input type="button" value="Sign In" />
        </td>
    </tr>
</table>

</body>
</html>
```

Creating Full-Screen Windows

Problem

For the purpose of enabling more viewing space or enabling additional interactions, your application needs to be able to run using the full screen.

Solution

The NativeWindow class provides the foundation for creating transparent and full screen.

Discussion

The differences between using NativeWindow for full-screen display, and using NativeWindow for custom windows, is an additional initialization option and setting the window to fill the screen. To remove any OS-specific windowing chrome, use the NativeWindowInitOptions.systemChrome property. The NativeWindowInitOptions.systemChrome should be set to one of the four string constants (Table 4-1) found in the NativeWindowSystemChrome class.

Table 4-1. String constants in NativeWindowSystemChrome

String constant	Description
`NativeWindowSystemChrome.STANDARD`	This is the default for `NativeWindow` and reflects the window chrome used on the specific operating system.
`NativeWindowSystemChrome.UTILITY`	Utility chrome is best suited for related windows that will be present for an extended amount of time such as tool panels.
`NativeWindowSystemChrome.NONE`	Indicates that no chrome should be present, and requires that the application handle all traditional windowing tasks.
`NativeWindowSystemChrome.ALTERNATE`	Not implemented for the Adobe AIR Beta.

To create a full-screen window without any chrome, the `NativeWindowInitOptions.systemChrome` property should be set to `NativeWindowSystemChrome.NONE`. The application can then subsequently call the `NativeWindow.maximize( )` method, or set `NativeWindow.bounds` directly. The `NativeWindow.bounds` property takes a `flash.geom.Rectangle` object which specifies horizontal and vertical origination, as well as width and height. Either approach fills the viewable screen with the newly created native window.

```
var options = new air.NativeWindowInitOptions( );
var login = null;

options.minimizable = false;
options.maximizable = false;
options.resizable = false;
options.systemChrome = air.NativeWindowSystemChrome.NONE;

login = new air.NativeWindow( false, options );
login.maximize( );
```

```html
<html>
<head>

<title>Full Screen Window</title>
<script type="text/javascript" src="AIRAliases.js">
</script>

<script>
var Rectangle = window.runtime.flash.geom.Rectangle;

function doLoad()
{
    var control = new window.runtime.flash.html.
HTMLControl();
    var options = new air.NativeWindowInitOptions();
    var win = null;

    options.minimizable = false;
    options.maximizable = false;
    options.resizable = false;
    options.systemChrome = air.NativeWindowSystemChrome.NONE;

    win = new air.NativeWindow( false, options );
    win.alwaysInFront = true;
    win.bounds = new Rectangle(
                0,
                0,
                air.Capabilities.screenResolutionX,
                air.Capabilities.screenResolutionY );
    win.visible = true;

    control.width = win.stage.stageWidth;
    control.height = win.stage.stageHeight;
  control.load( new air.URLRequest( "http://www.adobe.com" ) );
```

```
    win.stage.scaleMode = window.runtime.flash.display.
StageScaleMode.NO_SCALE;
    win.stage.align = window.runtime.flash.display.
StageAlign.TOP_LEFT;
    win.stage.addChild( control );
}
</script>

</head>
<body onload="doLoad( )">


</body>
</html>
```

File API

Writing Text to a File from a String

Problem

A user has made changes to textual content in the application, which the user wants to save to disk for offline access.

Solution

Writing text can be accomplished through the File and FileStream classes that are part of AIR.

Discussion

Before any reading or writing takes place to disk, a reference to a file or directory must first exist in the application. A file reference can be established in a number of ways, including programmatic manipulation and user selection. Both of these are accomplished by using the File class. The File class also contains static properties that point to common locations on the operating system. These locations include the desktop directory, user directory and documents directory:

```
var file =
air.File.applicationStorageDirectory.resolve( "myFile.txt" );
```

The call to File.resolve( ) creates a reference to a file named
myFile.txt located in the application storage directory. Once
a reference has been established, it can be used in file IO
operations. Note that this doesn't actually create the file at
this point.

Physically reading and writing to disk is available using the
FileStream class. The FileStream class does not take any
arguments in its constructor:

```
var stream = new air.FileStream( );
```

With the file reference available, and a FileStream object
instantiated, the process of writing data to disk can take
place. The type of data that can be written may be anything
from binary, to text, to value objects. These can all be
accessed by using the respective FileStream method for that
operation.

The first step in writing a file is to open it using the
FileStream.open( ) method. The FileStream.open( ) method
takes two arguments. The first argument is the file reference
created earlier that will be the destination of the output. The
second argument is the type of access the application will
need to the file. In the case of writing data to a file, the
FileMode.WRITE static property will be most common. A
second possibility is FileMode.APPEND, depending on the
application requirements:

```
stream.open( file, air.FileMode.WRITE );
```

When writing text, an application should use FileStream.
writeMultiByte( ) to ensure that data is written with the correct encoding. The FileStream.writeMultiByte( ) method
takes two arguments. The first argument is the String object
(text) that will be written to disk. The second argument is the
character set to be used. The most common character set is

that which the operating system is using, which is available on the File class as File.systemCharset:

```
stream.writeMultiByte( document.getElementById
( "txtNote" ).value, air.File.systemCharset );
```

Once the text has been written to the file, it is important to close the file to avoid any corruption or blocking of access from other applications. Closing a file is accomplished using the FileStream.close( ) method.

TIP

XML data is already in textual format and, as such, can be written to disk using these same series of steps. If the application uses the XMLHttpRequest object, then a using the myXml.responseText property alone may be adequate for most situations.

```
<html>
<head>

<title>Write Text</title>
<script type="text/javascript" src="AIRAliases.js"></
script>

<script>
function doLoad( )
{
    document.getElementById( "btnSave" ).addEventListener
    ( "click", doSave );
}

function doSave( )
{
    var file =
air.File.applicationResourceDirectory.resolve( "note.txt" );
    var stream = new air.FileStream( );

    stream.open( file, air.FileMode.WRITE );
    stream.writeMultiByte( document.getElementById
    ( "txtNote" ).value, air.File.systemCharset );
    stream.close( );
}
</script>
```

```
    </head>
    <body onload="doLoad( )">

    <textarea id="txtNote"></textarea>
    <input id="btnSave" type="button" value="Save" />

    </body>
    </html>
```

Synchronously Reading Text from a File

Problem

You want to read the contents of a small text file into your application.

Solution

Use the various file APIs provided by Adobe AIR to locate, open, and read text files.

Discussion

Small files that contain text content can be read using the FileStream.open( ) method. This method opens a file synchronously for reading. Synchronous access requires less code, but also blocks any additional user input until the data has been read. When using asynchronous access, additional user input is not blocked, but event handlers must be registered, which results in more code overhead.

TIP

While accessing XML files as text is possible, the result of this approach is a document object that can't be readily manipulated. Accessing an XML file for use as a data source, is often more easily handled using XMLHttpRequest or wrapper functionality offered by most JavaScript libraries.

The steps for synchronously reading a file are almost always the same:

1. Get a File reference
2. Create a FileStream object
3. Open the stream for synchronous access
4. Call the appropriate FileStream read methods
5. Close the file

The first step to reading a text file is to get a reference to the resource on disk. Establishing a reference can be accomplished by programmatically designating a path using the appropriate property on the File object such as File.applicationStorageDirectory. Calling File.resolve( ) will also be required when using this approach as the static File class properties always return a directory:

```
var file =
air.File.applicationStorageDirectory.resolve( "myFile.txt" );
```

The FileStream class has an empty constructor and can be instantiated anywhere in your application. The file reference just established is used during the physical process of opening the file. The mode for which the file is going to be opened must also be specified.

The FileMode object serves no other purpose but to provide constants for the types of file access that can be performed. These operations are FileMode.READ, FileMode.WRITE, FileMode.UPDATE and FileMode.APPEND:

```
var stream = new air.FileStream( );
stream.open( file, air.FileMode.READ );
```

There are three FileStream methods that can be used to read character data from a file. The FileStream.readUTF( ) and FileStream.readUTFBytes( ) methods are specifically tuned for UTF data.

If this is the target format of the data for the application, then these methods should be used directly. In the case of other character sets, the `FileStream.readMultiBytes()` method can be used to specify the target format. Additional character sets are specified in the form of a string such as "us-ascii". There is also a convenience property on the File object to use the default system character set, `File.systemCharset`.

The number of bytes to be read also needs to be specified in the case of `FileStream.readUTFBytes()` and `FileStream.readMultiBytes()`. This sizing will depend largely on the requirements of the application. In the cases where reading the entire file is required, the number of bytes that are available to be read can be found on the `FileStream.bytesAvailable` property:

```
var data =
stream.readMultiBytes( stream.bytesAvailable,
                       air.File.systemCharset );
```

Once the contents of a file have been read, it is important to close the file. This operation will allow other applications to access the file:

```
stream.close();
```

Although a demonstrable amount of flexibility has been provided by Adobe AIR, the actual process in its entirety is considerably concise. This brevity is provided when performing synchronous data access operations. Synchronous file access should be reserved for smaller files regardless of reading or writing character or binary data:

```
<html>
<head>

<title>Synchronous File Access</title>
<script type="text/javascript" src="AIRAliases.js"></
script>

<script>
var file = null;
var stream = null;
```

```
function doLoad( )
{
    var data = null;

    file = air.File.applicationStorageDirectory.resolve(
"myFile.txt" );

    stream = new air.FileStream( );
    stream.open( file, air.FileMode.READ );
    data = stream.readMultiByte( stream.bytesAvailable,
air.File.systemCharset );
    stream.close( );

    document.getElementById( "editor" ).value = data;
}
</script>

</head>
<body onload="doLoad( )">

<textarea id="editor"></textarea>

</body>
</html>
```

Asynchronously Reading Text from a File

Problem

You want to read a large amount of text into your application.

Solution

Use asynchronous file APIs to load the text, ensuring application execution is not blocked while the file is being loaded.

Discussion

Files containing a large amount of data should be read using the FileStream.openAsync( ) method. This method opens a file asynchronously for reading or writing and won't block additional user input. Asynchronous file operations achieve this goal by raising events during processing. The result is that event listeners must be created and registered on the FileStream object.

The steps for asynchronously reading a file are almost always the same:

1. Get a File reference
2. Create a FileStream object
3. Create event handlers for processing data
4. Add event listeners for asynchronous operations
5. Open the stream for asynchronous access
6. Close the file

The first step to reading a text file is to get a reference to the resource on disk. Establishing a reference can be accomplished by programmatically designating a path using the appropriate property on the File object such as File.applicationStorageDirectory:

```
var file =
air.File.applicationStorageDirectory.resolve( "myFile.txt" );
```

A FileStream instance is necessary in order to read or write to the file:

```
stream = new air.FileStream( );
```

Before registering event handlers on a FileStream object, those handlers will need to be created. The events that are triggered by file IO operations using the FileStream class will always pass an event object as an argument. The properties on the event object will depend on the type of event being raised. This object can be helpful in determining the target FileStream object, how much data is available for reading, how much data is waiting to be written, and so on:

```
function doProgress( event )
{
    // Read all the data that is currently available
    var data = stream.readMultiByte( stream.
bytesAvailable, air.File.systemCharset );
```

```
    // Append the most recent content
    document.getElementById( "editor" ).value += data;

    // Close the file after the entire contents have been
read
    if( event.bytesLoaded == event.bytesTotal )
    {
        stream.close( );
    }
}
```

Registering for events takes place using the addEventListener( ) API:

```
stream.addEventListener( air.ProgressEvent.PROGRESS,
doProgress );
```

Opening a stream for asynchronous access is accomplished using the FileStream.openAsync( ). The FileStream. openAsync( ) method takes two arguments that specify the file being accessed and the type of access being performed.

The FileMode object serves no other purpose but to provide constants for the types of file access that can be performed. These operations are FileMode.READ, FileMode.WRITE, FileMode.UPDATE, and FileMode.APPEND:

```
stream.openAsync( file, air.FileMode.READ );
```

As soon as the file is opened and new data is available in the stream, the ProgressEvent.PROGRESS event is triggered. Depending on the size of the file, as well as machine and network characteristics, not all the bytes may be read in a single pass. In many cases, additional read operations take place, raising a ProgressEvent.PROGRESS event for each iteration.

Once all of the data has been read from the file, an Event. COMPLETE event is broadcast.

Once the file has been read, it is important to close the file stream in order to ensure that other applications can access it:

```
stream.close( );
```

This example provides a baseline for the various types of asynchronous access an application might choose to perform. In this case, the contents of the file are read and placed into an HTML text area each time more data is available. Asynchronous processing also provides the means for random file access (seek) without interrupting the user. An application should always use asynchronous access whenever the size of a file is in question:

```
<html>
<head>

<title>Asynchronous File Access</title>
<script type="text/javascript" src="AIRAliases.js"></script>

<script>
var file = null;
var stream = null;

function doLoad()
{
    file = air.File.applicationStorageDirectory.resolve(
"myFile.txt" );

    stream = new air.FileStream();
    stream.addEventListener( air.ProgressEvent.PROGRESS,
                             doProgress );
    stream.openAsync( file, air.FileMode.READ );
}

function doProgress( event )
{
    var data = stream.readMultiByte( stream.
bytesAvailable, air.File.systemCharset );

    document.getElementById( "editor" ).value += data;

    if( event.bytesLoaded == event.bytesTotal )
    {
        stream.close();
    }
}
</script>
```

```
</head>
<body onload="doLoad()">

<textarea id="editor"></textarea>

</body>
</html>
```

Loading Data from an XML File

Problem

You want to read XML data from a local file using common
JavaScript techniques, and be able to manipulate the DOM
not just the character data.

Solution

Reading a local XML document for the data can occur using
the XMLHttpRequest object, and by using a File object reference as the URI endpoint as opposed to a web address.

Discussion

Most JavaScript libraries, and virtually every data-oriented
Ajax application uses the XMLHttpRequest object to load data.
This is a common means to accessing data from the client
without refreshing the page, and is core to Ajax develop-
ment techniques. Adobe AIR includes support for the
XMLHttpRequest object, which can be used for data access.

The XMLHttpRequest.open() method expects three arguments.
The first argument is the HTTP method to be used for the call,
which is commonly GET or POST. The third argument tells
the object whether or not it should make the request asynchronously. The challenge in an AIR application is the second
argument that tells the object where to get its data:

```
XMLHttpRequest.open( "GET", "myData.xml", true );
```

This URI endpoint generally points to a remote server. This
can still happen in an application that is online, but as AIR

---

applications can also work offline, the endpoint needs to be pointed to a local resource. Rather than pass an endpoint to a remote server, a File reference can be provided:

```
var file = air.File.applicationStorageDirectory.resolve(
"myData.xml" );
var xml = new XMLHttpRequest();

xml.onreadystatechange = function()
{
    if( xml.readystate == 4 )
    {
    // Work with data
    }
}

xml.open( "GET", file.url, true );
xml.send( null );
```

The key distinction to make for this example is the use of the File.url property, which the XMLHttpRequest object understands and uses to access the appropriate data. Using this approach results in a traditional DOM that can be used to traverse and manipulate the XML data in the file. Additionally, this approach can be used with common JavaScript libraries.

Given

```
<rolodex>
    <contact>
        <first>Kevin</first>
        <last>Hoyt</last>
    </contact>
    ...
</rolodex>
```

Example

```
<html>
<head>

<title>XML File Access</title>
<script type="text/javascript" src="AIRAliases.js">
</script>
```

```
<script>
var file = null;
var xml = null;

function doLoad()
{
    file = air.File.applicationResourceDirectory;
    file = file.resolve( "rolodex.xml" );

    xml = new XMLHttpRequest();

    xml.onreadystatechange = function()
    {
        var elem = null;
        var first = null;
        var last = null;
        var rolodex = null;

        if( xml.readyState == 4 )
        {
            rolodex = xml.responseXML.documentElement.
getElementsByTagName( "contact" );

            for( var c = 0; c < rolodex.length; c++ )
            {
                first = rolodex[c].getElementsByTagName(
"first" )[0].textContent;
                last = rolodex[c].getElementsByTagName(
"last" )[0].textContent;

                elem = document.createElement( "div" );
                elem.innerText = first + " " + last;
                document.body.appendChild( elem );
            }
        }
    }

    xml.open( "GET", file.url, true );
    xml.send( null );
}
</script>

</head>
<body onload="doLoad()">

</body>
</html>
```

Creating a Temporary File

Problem

An application needs to store transient information during file processing, and cannot assume that adequate memory exists to store the data in memory.

Solution

Creating temporary files with `File.createTempFile()` is an ideal means to store transient information while relieving the overhead of additional memory.

Discussion

The File class contains a static `File.createTempFile()` method which can be used to establish a temporary file. The temporary file is created at a destination determined by the operating system. Temporary files are also automatically given a unique name to avoid collision with other files that may be present:

```
var temp = air.File.createTempFile();
```

Once a temporary file has been created, the other `File` and `FileStream` methods may be used as in processing a known file at a known location:

```
var stream = new air.FileStream();

stream.open( temp, air.FileMode.WRITE );
stream.writeMultiByte( "Hello", air.File.systemCharset );
stream.close();
```

The `File.moveTo()` and `File.moveToAsync()` can be used after the fact, should you decide that it is necessary to keep the temporary file for later reference. Both move methods take two arguments. The first argument is a File reference to the destination location. The second argument is a Boolean value which controls overwriting any existing file. If the second argument is set to false, and a collision occurs, the application throws an error:

```
var move =
air.File.applicationResourceDirectory.resolve( "temp.txt" );

try
{
    temp.moveTo( move, false );
}
catch( ioe )
{
    alert( "Can't move file:\n" + ioe.message );
}
```

The JavaScript try/catch block will receive an error object of type IOError. The IOError class has numerous properties available that can be used for further evaluation. The exception in the previous code snippet raises the error message that is generated by Adobe AIR:

```
<html>
<head>

<title>Temporary File</title>
<script type="text/javascript" src="AIRAliases.js"></
script>

<script>
function doLoad( )
{
    var stream = new air.FileStream( );
    var temp = air.File.createTempFile( );
    var move = air.File.applicationResourceDirectory.
resolve( "temp.txt" );

    stream.open( temp, air.FileMode.WRITE );
    stream.writeMultiByte( "Hello", air.File.systemCharset
);
    stream.close( );

    try
    {
        temp.moveTo( move, false );
    }
```

```
      catch( ioe )
      {
          alert( "Could not move temporary file:\n" + ioe.message );
      }
   }
</script>

</head>
<body onload="doLoad( )">


</body>
</html>
```

Iterate the Contents of a Directory

Problem

The application is required to display information about a
directory as part of the user interface.

Solution

Use the File.browseForDirectory API to prompt the user to
select a directory, and then use the File.listDirectory API
to iterate through the contents of the directory.

Discussion

The File class provides numerous properties that can be used
to get specific information about files on disk. There are also
two methods on the File class that pertain to getting a directory list. The first is the File.browseForDirectory( ), which
can be used to prompt the user to select a directory using the
native dialog. The second is the File.listDirectory( )
method, which will return an array of File objects for the
currently referenced directory.

Before prompting the user to select a directory using the
native dialog, the application needs to establish and register
an event handler for Event.SELECT. The Event.target

property will contain a reference to the File object the invoked the browse operation:

```
var directory = air.File.documentsDirectory;
directory.addEventListener( air.Event.SELECT, doSelect );
directory.browseForDirectory( "Select a directory of
photos:" );
```

The File.browseForDirectory( ) method takes one argument, a string representing additional information that will be placed in the dialog box. This string is not the title of the dialog as is the case with File.browseForOpen( ). There is also no need to specify FileFilter objects as the dialog box presented is specific to directories, and no files will be displayed.

After the user has selected a directory, the registered event handler will be called. The file reference, whether using a class/global reference or Event.target, will now contain the path to the selected directory. This is where File. listDirectory( ) comes into play as it returns an Array of File objects for the selected directory (as represented by the file reference). The File.listDirectory( ) method takes no arguments:

```
var listing = directory.listDirectory( );
```

The File class can represent both files and directories on the user's file system. The File.isDirectory API can be used to determine whether a specific File instance references a file or a directory.

TIP

See the API documentation for a complete list of data exposed by the File API.

```
<html>
<head>

<title>Get a Directory Listing</title>
<script type="text/javascript" src="AIRAliases.js">
</script>
```

```
<script>
var directory = null;

function doBrowse()
{
    directory.browseForDirectory( "Select a directory of files:" )
}

function doLoad()
{
    directory = air.File.documentsDirectory;
    directory.addEventListener( air.Event.SELECT,
                                doSelect );

    document.getElementById( "btnBrowse" ).
addEventListener( "click", doBrowse );
}

function doSelect( event )
{
    var files = directory.listDirectory();
    var elem = null;
    var name = null;
    var mod = null;
    var size = null;

    for( var f = 0; f < files.length; f++ )
    {
        name = files[f].name;

        mod = files[f].modificationDate;
        mod = ( mod.month + 1 ) + "/" +
                mod.date + "/" +
                mod.fullYear;

      size = Math.ceil( files[f].size / 1000 ) + " KB";

        elem = document.createElement( "div" );
        elem.innerText = name + " is " +
      size + " and was last modified on " +
      mod;

        document.body.appendChild( elem );
    }
}
</script>
```

```
        </head>
        <body onload="doLoad( )">

        <input id="btnBrowse" type="button" value="Browse" />

        </body>
        </html>
```

File Pickers

Browse for a File

Problem

An application needs to prompt the user to select a file to
open from the local system using a native dialog.

Solution

The File class allows an application to prompt the user to
select one or more files of a specific type from the local
system.

Discussion

The File class provides numerous browse methods that
present the native dialog for the specified operation. In the
case of browsing for a single file to open, the appropriate
method is File.browseForOpen( ). This method takes a
required string argument for the title of the dialog box, and
an optional Array of FileFilter objects.

FileFilter objects allow an application to filter the viewable
files in the native dialog box. This argument is null by
default, which allows the user to select any file to which they
would normally have access (i.e., not hidden files). An application can provide as many filters as necessary, by placing
multiple FileFilter objects in an Array and passing that
Array as the second argument to File.browseForOpen( );.

If you want to use the FileFilter object, you must use the Array class from the Flash runtime, not the JavaScript Array class.

None of the browse methods on the File class are static, and as such, an existing reference to a valid File object must first be available. The directory represented by that File object reference will be selected by default when the dialog is displayed:

```
var file = air.File.documentsDirectory;
var filters = new window.runtime.Array( );

filters.push( new FileFilter( "Image Files", "*.jpg" ) );
file.browseForOpen( file, filters );
```

When a file selection has been made, Adobe AIR will raise an event in the issuing application. In order to catch that event, the application must have first registered an event listener. The event that gets raised is Event.SELECT, and an Event object will be passed to the handler:

```
var file = air.File.documentsDirectory;
var filters = new window.runtime.Array( );

filters.push( new air.FileFilter( "Image Files", "*.jpg" )
);

file.addEventListener( air.Event.SELECT, doSelect );
file.browseForOpen( file, filters );

function doSelect( event )
{
    alert( file.nativePath );
}
```

A useful property of the Event object that is sent to the handler is the "target," which contains a reference to the originating File object. There is nothing returned from the dialog operation to be assigned to a File object, as the originating object will now hold a reference to the directory selected by the user. For this purpose, it may be beneficial to have a class or global reference to the File object, and even to reuse it:

```
<html>
<head>

<title>Browse for a File</title>
<script type="text/javascript" src="AIRAliases.js">
</script>

<script>
var file = null;

function doLoad( )
{
    file = air.File.documentsDirectory;
    file.addEventListener( air.Event.SELECT, doSelect );

    document.getElementById( "btnBrowse" ).
    addEventListener( "click", doBrowse );
}

function doBrowse( )
{
    var filters = new window.runtime.Array( );

    filters.push( new air.FileFilter( "Image Files", "*.jpg" )
);
    file.browseForOpen( "Select Photo", filters );
}

function doSelect( event )
{
    var elem = document.createElement( "div" );

    elem.innerText = file.nativePath;
    document.body.appendChild( elem );
}
</script>

</head>
<body onload="doLoad( )">

<input id="btnBrowse" type="button" value="Browse" />

</body>
</html>
```

Browse for Multiple Files

Problem

An application needs to prompt the user to select multiple files from the local system using the native dialog.

Solution

Use the `File.browseForOpenMultiple()` API to prompt the user with a dialog box that will allow them to select multiple files.

Discussion

The use of the `File` class to open a single file is predominantly the same as using the `File` class to open multiple files. In the case of allowing the user to select multiple files, the appropriate method to use is `File.browseForOpenMultiple()`. The `File.browseForOpenMultiple()` method takes the same two arguments that the `File.browseForOpen()` method takes: a String to be used in the title of the dialog, and an Array of `FileFilter` objects.

Once the user has selected the files from the dialog, the `FileListEvent.SELECT_MULTIPLE` will be broadcast. The event object that is sent to the handler will be of type `FileListEvent`. The `FileListEvent` class contains a "files" property, which will be an `Array` of `File` objects representing the files that the user selected:

```
var file = air.File.documentsDirectory;

file.addEventListener( air.FileListEvent.SELECT_MULTIPLE,
doSelect );

function doSelect( event )
{
    for( var f = 0; f < event.files.length; f++ )
    {
        ...
    }
}
```

Here is the complete code:

```html
<html>
<head>

<title>Browse for Multiple Files</title>
<script type="text/javascript" src="AIRAliases.js">
</script>

<script>
var file = null;

function doLoad()
{
    file = air.File.documentsDirectory;
    file.addEventListener( air.FileListEvent.SELECT_MULTIPLE,
                           doSelect );

    document.getElementById( "btnBrowse" ).
addEventListener( "click", doBrowse );
}

function doBrowse()
{
    var filters = new window.runtime.Array();

    filters.push( new air.FileFilter( "Image Files", "*.jpg" ) );
    file.browseForOpenMultiple( "Select Photos", filters );
}

function doSelect( event )
{
    var elem = null;
    var name = null;
    var size = null;

    for( var f = 0; f < event.files.length; f++ )
    {
        name = event.files[f].name;
        size = Math.ceil( event.files[f].size / 1000 );

        elem = document.createElement( "div" );
        elem.innerText = name + " (" + size + " KB)";

        document.body.appendChild( elem );
    }
```

```
    }
    </script>

    </head>
    <body onload="doLoad()">

    <input id="btnBrowse" type="button" value="Browse" />

    </body>
    </html>
```

Browse for a Directory

Problem

Application requirements dictate that you allow users to select a directory in which they will store data.

Solution

Use the `File.browseForDirectory()` API to prompt the user to select a directory.

Discussion

The `File.browseForDirectory()` API creates a native dialog box that allows users to select a directory. The method takes a required String argument, which will be used to provide additional information to the user about the purpose of the selected directory.

When a directory selection has been made, Adobe AIR will raise an event in the issuing application. In order to catch that event, the application must have first registered an event listener. The event that gets raised is `Event.SELECT`, and an event object will be passed to the handler:

```
var file = air.File.applicationStorageDirectory;

file.addEventListener( air.Event.SELECT, doSelect );
file.browseForDirectory( "Where do you want to store your
photos?" );

function doSelect( event )
```

```
    {
        alert( file.nativePath );
    }
```

A useful property of the event object that is sent to the handler is the target property that contains a reference to the originating File object. There is nothing returned from the dialog operation to be assigned to a File object, as the originating object will now hold a reference to the directory selected by the user. For this purpose, it may be beneficial to have a class or global reference to the File object, and even to reuse it:

```
<html>
<head>

<title>Select Directory</title>
<script type="text/javascript" src="AIRAliases.js">
</script>

<script>
var file = null;

function doLoad( )
{
    file = air.File.documentsDirectory;
    file.addEventListener( air.Event.SELECT, doSelect );

    document.getElementById( "btnBrowse" ).
addEventListener( "click", doBrowse );
}

function doBrowse( )
{
file.browseForDirectory( "Where do you want to put your photos?" );
}

function doSelect( )
{
    var elem = document.createElement( "div" );

    elem.innerText = file.nativePath;
    document.body.appendChild( elem );
}
</script>
```

```
    </head>
    <body onload="doLoad( )">

    <input id="btnBrowse" type="button" value="Browse" />

    </body>
    </html>
```

Service and Server Monitoring

Monitoring Connectivity to an HTTP Server

Problem

Your application needs to monitor and determine whether a specific HTTP server can be reached.

Solution

Use the URLMonitor class to detect network state changes in HTTP/S endpoints.

Discussion

Service monitor classes work through event notification and subsequent polling of the designated endpoint. Service monitoring is not part of the Adobe Integrated Runtime (AIR) directly, and needs to be added before it can be used.

The classes for service monitoring are contained in the *servicemonitor.swf* file which can be found in the "frameworks" directory of the AIR SDK. This file should be copied into the application project folder, and can be included through the use of the HTML SCRIPT tag. The *servicemonitor.swf* file also needs to be included in the packaged AIR application.

```
    <script src="servicemonitor.swf"></script>
```

The URLMonitor class takes a single argument in the constructor, an instance of the URLRequest class. The URLRequest constructor takes a String that represents the URL service endpoint to query. The URLRequest class also contains information about how to query the endpoint (i.e. GET, POST), and any additional data that should be passed to the server:

```
var request = air.URLRequest( "http://www.adobe.com" ) ;
var monitor = new window.runtime.air.net.URLMonitor( request );
```

The URLMonitor class will raise a StatusEvent.STATUS event when the network state changes. Once the event handler has been registered, the URLMonitor instance can be told to start watching for network start changes:

```
monitor.addEventListener( air.StatusEvent.STATUS, doStatus );
monitor.start();
```

After a network change has been propagated as an event, the URLMonitor.available property on the originating URLMonitor instance can be used to check for the presence of a connection. The URLMonitor.available property returns a Boolean value that reflects the state of the network. As it is necessary to query the originating URLMonitor instance for network availability, the object should be declared in a scope that is accessible across the application:

```
<html>
<head>

<title>HTTP Monitor</title>
<script type="text/javascript" src="AIRAliases.js">
</script>
<script src="servicemonitor.swf"></script>

<script>
var monitor = null;

function doLoad( )
{
    var request = new air.URLRequest( "http://www.adobe.
com" );

    monitor = new window.runtime.air.net.URLMonitor( request );
    monitor.addEventListener( air.StatusEvent.STATUS, doStatus );
    monitor.start( );
}
```

```
function doStatus( event )
{
    var elem = document.createElement( "div" );

    elem.innerText = monitor.available;

    document.body.appendChild( elem );
}
</script>

</head>
<body onload="doLoad( )">

</body>
</html>
```

Monitoring Connectivity to a Jabber Server

Problem

A Jabber chat client is required to reflect network presence in
the user interface, but the endpoint is a Jabber server on a
specific port and not HTTP/S.

Solution

Use the SocketMonitor class to detect network state changes
against TCP/IP socket endpoints.

Discussion

The service monitoring API is not built into Adobe AIR
directly, and needs to be added before it can be used. The
servicemonitor.swf file, which is included in the Adobe AIR
SDK, must be included as an application resource and
included via an HTML SCRIPT tag:

```
<script src="servicemonitor.swf"></script>
```

The SocketMonitor class takes two arguments in the constructor: a String that represents the host endpoint, and a
port on which the server is listening:

```
var host = "im.mydomain.com";
var port = 5220;
```

```
var monitor =
  new window.runtime.air.net.SocketMonitor( host, port );
```

The SocketMonitor class will raise a StatusEvent.STATUS event when the network state changes. Once the event handler has been registered, calling the SocketMonitor.start( ) method will start watching the network for changes:

```
monitor.addEventListener( air.StatusEvent.STATUS, doStatus );
monitor.start( );
```

After a network change has been propagated as an event, the SocketMonitor.available property on the originating SocketMonitor instance can be used to check for the presence of a connection. The SocketMonitor.available property returns a Boolean value that reflects the state of the network. As a best practice, the SocketMonitor object should be declared in a scope that is accessible across the application and referenced directly during event handling:

```
<html>
<head>

<title>Socket Monitor</title>
<script type="text/javascript" src="AIRAliases.js">
</script>
<script src="servicemonitor.swf"></script>

<script>
var monitor = null;

function doLoad( )
{
    monitor = new window.runtime.air.net.Socket
Monitor( "im.mydomain.com", 5220 );
  monitor.addEventListener( air.StatusEvent.STATUS, doStatus );
    monitor.start( );
}

function doStatus( event )
{
    var elem = document.createElement( "div" );

    elem.innerText = monitor.available;
```

```
      document.body.appendChild( elem );
}
</script>

</head>
<body onload="doLoad( )">

</body>
</html>
```

Online/Offline

Caching Assets for Offline Use

Problem

You want to load an asset from a URL and store it for use
when the application is offline.

Solution

Use the File I/O API to save the requested asset to the application's store and read that file on subsequent requests.

Discussion

In this example, we will load an XML file that is at a known
URL. Once the data has been loaded, it will be saved to the
local disk and on subsequent requests for the document, it
will be loaded from the local disk instead of from the remote
location.

First, we will use the XMLHttpRequest object to load the XML
data from the remote location. The XMLHTTPRequest.open( )
method takes three arguments. The first argument is the
method of the HTTP request that is being made. The second
argument is the URI of the location of the data being loaded.
The third argument is a Boolean that specifies whether the
operation will be asynchronous.

Once we have specified these arguments in the open method, we will call the send method. The send method takes a single argument that contains the content that is to be sent with the request. In our case, we won't send any data with the request:

```
var xml = new XMLHttpRequest();
xml.open( "GET", "http://www.foo.com/data.xml", true );
xml.send( null );
```

Because we are loading the data asynchronously, we need to create a handler for the response which is called once the data has loaded from the server. This handler will be added before the send method is called. Within this handler we will save the data that is located in the responseText property of the XMLHttpRequest instance to a known location on the local file system for retrieval in subsequent requests. Reading and writing text to the local system is covered elsewhere in the book, and therefore we won't cover it in detail here:

```
xml.onreadystatechange = function()
{
    if( xml.readyState == 4 ) // the request is complete
    {
        // write the data to the local system
      var file =
      air.File.applicationStorageDirectory.resolve("data.xml");
        var fileStream = new air.FileStream();
        fileStream.open( file, air.FileMode.WRITE );
        fileStream.writeMultiByte( xml.responseText ,
                                   air.File.systemCharset );
        fileStream.close();
    }
}
```

Before each request of the data we will need to check if the *data.xml* file exists. If it exists, we do not need to load the file using the XMLHttpRequest object and can use the File API to load it from the disk. This allows us to load the data even if the user is not currently online:

```
var data = null;
var file = air.File.applicationStorageDirectory.
resolve("data.xml");
```

```
    if( file.exists )
    {
        var fileStream = new air.FileStream( );
        fileStream.open( file, air.FileMode.READ );
        data =
        fileStream.readMultiByte( fileStream.bytesAvailable,
                                  air.File.systemCharset );
        fileStream.close( );
    }
    else
    {
        // read the data via XMLHttpRequest and write that
        // data to the file system
    }
```

Here is the complete example:

```
<html>
<head>
    <title>Caching Assets for Offline Use</title>
    <script src="AIRAliases.js"></script>
    <script>

        var file =
        air.File.applicationStorageDirectory.resolve("data.xml");

        function onLoad( )
        {
            if( file.exists )
            {
                var fileStream = new air.FileStream( );
                fileStream.open( file, air.FileMode.READ );
                document.getElementById( "dataText" ).value =
                    fileStream.readMultiByte(
                        fileStream.bytesAvailable,
                        air.File.systemCharset );
                fileStream.close( );
            }
            else
            {
                var xml = new XMLHttpRequest( );
                xml.open( "GET",
                        "http://www.foo.com/data.xml", true );

                xml.onreadystatechange = function( )
                {
```

```
                        if( xml.readyState == 4 ) // the
request is complete
                        {
                            var file = air.File.
applicationStorageDirectory.resolve("data.xml");
                            var fileStream = new air.
FileStream( );
                            fileStream.open( file, air.
FileMode.WRITE );
                            fileStream.writeMultiByte( xml.
responseText , air.File.systemCharset );
                            fileStream.close( );

                            document.getElementById(
"dataText" ).value = xml.responseText;
                        }
                    }

                    xml.send( null );
                }
            }
        </script>
    </head>
    <body onload="onLoad( )">
        <textarea id="dataText"></textarea>
    </body>
    </html>
```

Drag and Drop

Using Drag and Drop from HTML

Problem

You want to allow users to drag files, images, text, and other data types into and out HTML-based AIR applications.

Solution

By using Adobe AIR's Drag and Drop implementation in JavaScript, developers can react to drag and drop operations that occur on HTML DOM objects.

Discussion

One of the benefits of developing for the desktop is providing users with a more integrated experience when interacting with multiple applications. One of the most frequently used user gestures is to drag and drop files, data, and other elements between applications and the desktop and between the applications themselves.

This example will demonstrate how you can accept text being dragged into your application and also support dragging text out. It will also show you how to modify the drag effect in order to demonstrate for the user what type of drag operations he can perform with the element he is dragging.

There are two flows that are important to consider when using drag and drop operations in HTML. First we will examine the flow for HTML elements that want to allow themselves to be dragged by users:

1. Element specifies that it is available for drag operations.
2. User selects the item and starts dragging it.
3. Element receives an `ondragstart` event and sets the data which will be transferred and also specifies which drag operations are supported.
4. Element receives `ondrag` events while the element is being dragged.
5. User drops the item being dragged and the initiating element receives an `ondragend` event.

The typical flow for HTML elements that want to receive drop operations are as follows:

1. User drags an item over the element listening for drop events.

2. Element receives an `ondragenter` event and specifies which drop operations are available.

3. Element receives `ondragover` operations continuously as the item is dragged over the element.

4. The user drops the item and the receiving element receives an `ondrop` event.

5. If the user moves the dragged item outside the boundaries of the listening element, it will receive an `ondragleave` event.

Users can, by default, drag text elements and URLs. To disable this functionality, use the `-khtml-user-drag:none` style. To override the default data type that is being specified, use the `-khtml-user-drag:element` style and specify listeners for the drag events as specified previously.

To manipulate the data that is being transferred between applications, use the `dataTransfer` object that is attached to the event dispatched during drag operations. The `dataTransfer` object has two methods, `getData` and `setData`. The `setData` method takes two parameters, the MIME type and the string of data that conforms to that type. The `setData` method can be called multiple times and allows you to store multiple data types. For example, if you wanted to specify a "text/plain" type and a "text/uri-list" type, you would do the following:

```
function dropStartListener( event )
{
    event.dataTransfer.setData( "text/plain", "Adobe" );
    event.dataTransfer.setData( "text/uri-list",
                                "http://www.adobe.com" );
}
```

If `setData` is called for a MIME type that already exists on the element being dragged, that data will be overwritten. Retrieving data from an element that is being dragged can occur only within an `ondrop` event handler. The `getData` method takes a MIME type as its only parameter and returns the value of the MIME type if it exists on the element being dragged. For example:

```
function dropListener( event )
{
    alert( event.dataTransfer.getData( "text/plain" ) );
    // Adobe
}
```

When a user is dragging an item from one application to another, or from one location in your application to another, you may want to indicate to the user which operations (copy, link, or move) are available. By using the `effectAllowed` and `dropEffect` properties of the `dataTransfer` object you can specify which operations are allowed. The system then uses the application to determine what actions a user can perform during the drag operation. The list of available values for these properties can be determined by reading the document referenced above.

When starting a drag, the `effectAllowed` property tells the system what operations the source element supports. The `dropEffect` property specifies the operation that the current target receiving the drag event supports. The system then uses the information about what effects both the source and destination target support and displays that to the user.

TIP

The current AIR Beta on Adobe Labs has a few limitations. First, specifying custom drag images and snapshots is not supported. Also, only two MIME types are available for transfer: text/plain, and text/uri-list. Last, the types array on the `dataTransfer` is not accessible on the `dataTransfer` object. Support for these features will be added for AIR Version 1.0.

```
<html>
<head>
    <title>HTML Drag Test</title>
    <script src="AIRAliases.js" />
    <script>

    // DROP EVENTS

    function onDragEnter(event)
    {
        air.trace("onDragEnter");
        event.dataTransfer.dropEffect = "copy";
        event.preventDefault();
    }

    function onDrop(event)
    {
      air.trace("onDrop");
      air.trace( event.dataTransfer.getData("text/plain") );
      air.trace( event.dataTransfer.getData("text/uri-list") );
    }

    function onDragOver(event)
    {
        event.preventDefault();
    }

    // DRAG EVENTS

    function onDragStart(event)
    {
        air.trace("onDragStart");
        event.dataTransfer.setData("text/plain",
           "This is the URL I am dragging" );
        // We overwrite the default URL specified in the
        // anchor tag with a different URL. When the data
        // is dropped, this is the URL that will be
        //  transferred.
        event.dataTransfer.setData("text/uri-list",
                                   "http://www.foo.com" );
        event.dataTransfer.effectAllowed = "all";
    }

    function onDragEnd( event )
    {
        air.trace("onDragEnd");
    }
```

```
        </script>
    </head>
    <body>
        <div style="margin: 0px auto; width: 80%;
        background-color: white; border: solid black;">
            <div style="background-color: lightblue;
            border-bottom: solid black; padding: 3px;
            font-family: sans-serif; font-weight: bold;"
                ondragenter="onDragEnter(event)"
                ondragover="onDragOver(event)"
                ondrop="onDrop(event)">
                Drop Here
            </div>
            <p>
                <span id="content" ondragstart="onDragStart(event)"
ondragend="onDragEnd(event)">
                <a href="http://www.adobe.com">Drag Me
                (text/uri-list)</a>
                </span>
            </p>
        </div>
    </body>
</html>
```

Embedded Database

Adobe AIR includes an embedded SQLite database which
can be leveraged by AIR applications. SQLite is a compact
open source database that supports ACID transactions,
requires zero-configuration, implements most of SQL92, and
supports strings and BLOBs up to 2GB in size. All database
information is stored in a single file on disk, and can be freely
shared between machines, even if they have different byte
orders.

TIP

You can find more information about SQLite on the
project web site at: *http://www.sqlite.org*.

Currently, when working with a local database from AIR, all transactions are asynchronous. This configuration allows the user interface to continue to respond while the database is processing in the background. To monitor database activity, an application must create and register for the events in which it is interested.

Connecting to a Database

Problem

You need to connect to a local database prior to working with the schema or altering data.

Solution

Creating and connecting to a database can be accomplished using the single SQLConnection.open() method.

Discussion

SQLite stores all database information in a single file on disk. This means that before an application can access a database, it must first have a reference to the file. A single application might choose to access any number of database files. Databases are managed through the SQLConnection datatype in the AIR API.

Obtaining a reference to the database file can be done through the File.resolve() method, which takes a single argument: the name of the file that will be referenced. Files that do not yet exist can have a reference, and the File. exists property returns a Boolean to determine that file's presence on disk:

```
var db = new air.SQLConnection();
var file =
 air.File.applicationStorageDirectory.resolve( "mycrm.db" );
```

The extension to the database file is not specific and can be named as necessary for the application.

Database transactions happen asynchronously, which means an application must first create and register a handler for the events in which it is interested. In the case of establishing a connection to a database, the SQLEvent.OPEN event will be monitored. Among various other properties, the SQLEvent.type property can be used to determine the status of the database.

```
db.addEventListener( air.SQLEvent.OPEN, doDbOpen );

function doDbOpen( event )
{
    alert( "Connected" );
}
```

Calling the SQLConnection.open() method can take a number of different arguments. The most common arguments are the file reference to the database, and a Boolean value indicating whether the database should be created if it does not already exist. This simultaneously creates the database if it does not exist, and then establishes a connection to the database:

```
db.open( file, true );
```

While the database will close automatically when the application exists, developers should consider calling SQLConnection.close() during the onunload event. The SQLConnection.close() method takes no arguments. Taking the time to manually close the database at the termination of the application helps ensure that data is not accidentally corrupted, and helps to maintain best practices:

```
<html>
<head>

<title>Connecting to a Database</title>
<script type="text/javascript" src="AIRAliases.js">
</script>

<script>
var db = new air.SQLConnection();

function doDbOpen( event )
```

```
{
    alert( "You are now connected to the database." );
}

function doLoad()
{
    var file =
    air.File.applicationResourceDirectory.resolve( "crm.db" );

    db.addEventListener( air.SQLEvent.OPEN, doDbOpen );
    db.open( file, true );
}

function doUnload()
{
    db.close();
}
</script>

</head>
<body onload="doLoad();" onunload="doUnload()">

</body>
</html>
```

Creating Database Tables

Problem

An application has a specific schema it needs to provide for data storage.

Solution

Database schema can be created using the SQLStatement class using SQL92.

Discussion

Once a database file has been created and a connection to the database has been established, the next likely step will be to create any required schema. This can be accomplished using SQL92 in conjunction with the SQLStatement class. The

`SQLStatement` class executes commands against a specified database.

As database transactions all happen asynchronously, the best place to check for any required schema—or to create it—is in the handler for the `SQLEvent.OPEN` event. At this point, the application can be assured a connection against which statements can be executed. Along the same lines, event handlers must also be registered on the `SQLStatement` instance:

```
var stmt = new air.SQLStatement();

stmt.addEventListener( air.SQLErrorEvent.ERROR,
  doStmtError );
stmt.addEventListener( air.SQLEvent.RESULT, doStmtResult );
```

When applied to a `SQLStatement` object, the `SQLErrorEvent.ERROR` event is called when there has been an error while executing a `SQLStatement.next()` or `SQLStatement.execute()` method. Conversely, the `SQLEvent.RESULT` event is called when results are returned from the database. This usually indicates a successful execution:

```
function doStmtError( event )
{
    alert( "There has been a problem executing the statement" );
}

function doStmtResult( event )
{
    alert( "The database table has been created." );
}
```

In order to execute a SQL statement, a `SQLConnection` instance against which to execute must be established. A `SQLConnection` instance can be assigned to the `SQLStatement.sqlConnection` property. The `SQLStatement.text` property is then assigned any SQL that needs to be executed. Finally, the `SQLStatement.execute()` method is called:

```
stmt.sqlConnection = db;
stmt.text = "CREATE TABLE IF NOT EXISTS contact ( " +
    "id INTEGER PRIMARY KEY AUTOINCREMENT, " +
    "first TEXT, " +
```

```
            "last TEXT )";
    stmt.execute();
```

In this case, a `CREATE TABLE` statement has been applied to the database. Additional types of SQL statements, such as `SELECT`, `INSERT`, `UPDATE`, and `DELETE` are executed in the same manner. The `SQLStatement.execute()` method can take two optional arguments: the number of rows to prefetch, and a responder object to handle events.

The prefetch option defaults to -1, which indicates that all rows should be returned. The responder object can be a custom object designed to handle any status or result events that take place during execution. The default responder is null in this case, as event handlers have been registered with the `SQLStatement` object directly:

```html
<html>
<head>

<title>Creating Database Tables</title>
<script type="text/javascript" src="AIRAliases.js">
</script>

<script>
var db = null;
var stmt = null

function doDbOpen( event )
{
    stmt = new air.SQLStatement();
    stmt.addEventListener( air.SQLErrorEvent.ERROR,
doStmtError );
    stmt.addEventListener( air.SQLEvent.RESULT,
doStmtResult );

    stmt.sqlConnection = db;
    stmt.text = "CREATE TABLE IF NOT EXISTS contact ( " +
                "id INTEGER PRIMARY KEY AUTOINCREMENT, " +
                "first TEXT, " +
                "last TEXT )";

    stmt.execute();
}
```

```
function doLoad()
{
    var file =
    air.File.applicationResourceDirectory.resolve( "crm.db" );

    db = new air.SQLConnection();
    db.addEventListener( air.SQLEvent.OPEN, doDbOpen );
    db.open( file, true );
}

function doStmtResult( event )
{
    alert( "The database table has been created." );
}

function doStmtError( event )
{
    alert( "There has been a problem executing a
    statement:\n" + event.error.message );
}

function doUnload()
{
    db.close();
}
</script>

</head>
<body onload="doLoad()" onunload="doUnload()">

</body>
</html>
```

Storing Data in a Database

Problem

An application needs to store user-provided data in a relational database on disk.

Solution

SQL92 INSERT statements can be created and executed using the SQLStatement class.

Discussion

Given a valid database file with the appropriate schema created, SQL92 statements can be executed using the SQLStatement object. The same SQLStatement object can be reused to execute multiple statements. When reusing the same SQLStatement, it's important to differentiate what type of statement has just been executed. There are various means to accomplish listening for the different actions.

```
function doSave( )
{
    var first = document.getElementById( "txtFirst" ).
value;
    var last = document.getElementById( "txtLast" ).value;

    stmt.text = "INSERT INTO contact VALUES ( " +
        "NULL, " +
        "'" + first + "', " +
        "'" + last + "' )";
    stmt.execute( );
}
```

One approach is to assign different event handlers for the different statements that will be executed. (Don't forget to remove the old handlers.) Another approach is to specify different responder objects that have been created with the specific statement in mind. The approach used in this example is a basic state machine that tracks what type of statement has just been executed:

```
var NONE = - 1;
var CREATE_SCHEMA = 0;
var INSERT_DATA = 1;

var state = NONE;

var stmt = new air.SQLStatement( );

// Other database creation and configuration

function doSave( )
{
    var first = document.getElementById( "txtFirst" ).value;
    var last = document.getElementById( "txtLast" ).value;
```

```
    stmt.text = "INSERT INTO contact VALUES ( " +
        "NULL, " +
    "'" + first + "', " +
        "'" + last + "' )";

    // Track state
    state = INSERT_DATA;
    stmt.execute();

}
```

After successfully executing a database statement, the SQLResultEvent.RESULT event will be triggered. If an error occurs, the SQLStatusEvent.STATUS event will be raised. By tracking the state, the method designed to handle the result can determine the appropriate action(s) to take. In the case of inserting new data, this may be user notification and updating of the user interface:

```
<html>
<head>

<title>Storing Database Data</title>
<script type="text/javascript" src="AIRAliases.js">
</script>

<script>
var db = null;
var stmt = null

var NONE = -1;
var CREATE_SCHEMA = 0;
var INSERT_DATA = 1;

var state = NONE;

function doDbOpen( event )
{
    stmt = new air.SQLStatement();
    stmt.addEventListener( air.SQLErrorEvent.ERROR,
                           doStmtError );
    stmt.addEventListener( air.SQLEvent.RESULT,
                           doStmtResult );

    stmt.sqlConnection = db;
    stmt.text = "CREATE TABLE IF NOT EXISTS contact ( " +
```

```
                    "id INTEGER PRIMARY KEY AUTOINCREMENT, " +
                    "first TEXT, " +
                    "last TEXT )";

    state = CREATE_SCHEMA;
    stmt.execute();
}

function doLoad()
{
    var file =
    air.File.applicationResourceDirectory.resolve( "crm.db" );

    db = new air.SQLConnection();
    db.addEventListener( air.SQLEvent.OPEN, doDbOpen );
    db.open( file, true );

    document.getElementById( "btnSave" ).
     addEventListener( "click", doSave );
}

function doSave()
{
    var first = document.getElementById( "txtFirst" ).value;
    var last = document.getElementById( "txtLast" ).value;

    stmt.text = "INSERT INTO contact VALUES ( " +
                "NULL, " +
                "'" + first + "', " +
                "'" + last + "' )";

    state = INSERT_DATA;
    stmt.execute();
}

function doStmtResult( event )
{
    switch( state )
    {
        case CREATE_SCHEMA:
            alert( "The database table has been created." );
            state = NONE;

            break;
```

```
            case INSERT_DATA:
            document.getElementById( "txtFirst" ).value = "";
            document.getElementById( "txtLast" ).value = "";

            alert( "A new record has been stored." );
    }
}

function doStmtError( event )
{
    alert( "There has been a problem executing a
statement:\n" + event.error.message );
}

function doUnload()
{
    db.close();
}
</script>

</head>
<body onload="doLoad()" onunload="doUnload()">

<div>
    First name: <input id="txtFirst" type="text" />
</div>
<div>
    Last name: <input id="txtLast" type="text" />
</div>
<div>
    <input id="btnSave" type="button" value="Save" />
</div>

</body>
</html>
```

Accessing Database Data

Problem

You need to generate a tabular display of data from the
embedded database.

Solution

Database data can be queried using SQL92 and the SQLStatement class.

Discussion

Traditional SELECT statements can be run using a SQLStatement object that has been referenced against an existing database. A successful execution of the SELECT statement invokes the registered SQLResultEvent.RESULT event handler. That event handler will get a SQLResultEvent object which contains the result data:

```
function doStmtResult( event )
{
    var elem = null;
    var results = stmt.getResult();

    if( results.data != null )
    {
        for( var c = 0; c < results.data.length; c++ )
{
    elem = document.createElement( "div" );
    elem.innerText = results.data[c].first + " "  +
results.data[c].last;

    document.body.appendChild( elem );
}
    }
}
```

TIP

This snippet forgoes much of the state management, event registration and database connectivity covered in other sections. Please review that content, or the example at the end of this section, for complete coverage of the topic.

To get any result data, the SQLStatement.getResult() is called, which returns a SQLResult object. The SQLResult.data property is an Array of the results, if any. The SQLResult.data

Array will contain Object instances whose properties match the names of the columns used in the query. This Array can be used to iterate over the results of a query.

If the database table that is being queried has no data, or the statement did not return any data, the SQLResult.data property will be null:

```
<html>
<head>

<title>Accessing Database Data</title>
<script type="text/javascript" src="AIRAliases.js">
</script>

<script>
var db = null;
var stmt = null

var NONE = -1;
var CREATE_SCHEMA = 0;
var SELECT_DATA = 1;

var state = NONE;

function doDbOpen( event )
{
    stmt = new air.SQLStatement();
    stmt.addEventListener( air.SQLErrorEvent.ERROR,
                        doStmtError );
    stmt.addEventListener( air.SQLEvent.RESULT,
                        doStmtResult );

    stmt.sqlConnection = db;
    stmt.text = "CREATE TABLE IF NOT EXISTS contact ( " +
                "id INTEGER PRIMARY KEY AUTOINCREMENT, " +
                "first TEXT, " +
                "last TEXT )";

    state = CREATE_SCHEMA;
    stmt.execute();
}

function doLoad()
{
```

```
    var file =
    air.File.applicationResourceDirectory.resolve( "crm.db" );

    db = new air.SQLConnection();
    db.addEventListener( air.SQLEvent.OPEN, doDbOpen );
    db.open( file, true );
}

function doStmtResult( event )
{
    var elem = null;
    var result = null;

    switch( state )

        case CREATE_SCHEMA:
            stmt.text = "SELECT * FROM contact";

            state = SELECT_DATA;
            stmt.execute();

            break;

        case SELECT_DATA:
            result = stmt.getResult();

            if( result.data != null )
            {
               for( var c = 0; c < result.data.length; c++ )
               {
                    elem = document.createElement( "div" );
                    elem.innerText = result.data[c].first +
                    " " + result.data[c].last;

                    document.body.appendChild( elem );
               }
            }

            state = NONE;
            break;

        default:
            state = NONE;
            break;
    }
}
```

```
function doStmtError( event )
{
    alert( "There has been a problem executing a
 statement:\n" + event.error.message );
}

function doUnload()
{
    db.close();
}
</script>

</head>
<body onload="doLoad()" onunload="doUnload()">

</body>
</html>
```

Command-Line Arguments

Capturing Command-Line Arguments

Problem

You need to capture command-line arguments sent to your application—either at application startup, or while the application is running.

Solution

Register for the InvokeEvent, and capture command line arguments passed into your application.

Discussion

Whenever an application is started, or an application is called from the command line while it is running, an InvokeEvent will be broadcast. The event handler for this is passed information about the event, including any arguments passed to the application on the command line.

You should register for the InvokeEvent during your application's initialization phase, in order to ensure that the event is captured when the application is initially launched.

You can register for the event from the shell singleton like so:

```
function init( )
{
  air.Shell.shell.addEventListener(air.InvokeEvent.INVOKE,
                                   onInvoke);
}
```

This registers the onInvoke function as a handler for the InvokeEvent. The handler is passed an instance of the InvokeEvent object, which contains a property named arguments which is an Array of Strings of any arguments passed to the application:

```
function onInvoke(event)
{
    air.trace("onInvoke : " + event.arguments);
}
```

When testing your application via ADL, you can pass in command line arguments by using the -- argument. For example:

```
adl InvokeExample.xml -- foo "bim bam"
```

This would pass in two arguments to the application "foo" and "bim bam."

The complete example follows; it listens for the InvokeEvent, and prints out to the included textarea html control, as well as the command line via air.trace( ):

```
<html>
<head>

    <script src="AIRAliases.js" />
    <script type="text/javascript">

      function onInvoke(event)
      {
        air.trace("onInvoke : " + event.arguments);
```

```
        var field = document.getElementById("outputField");
        field.value += "Invoke : " + event.arguments + "\n";
        }

        function init()
        {
            air.Shell.shell.addEventListener(air.
InvokeEvent.INVOKE,onInvoke);
        }

    </script>

</head>

<body onload="init()">

    <textarea rows="8" cols="40" id="outputField">
    </textarea>

</body>
</html>
```

Networking

Communicating on a Socket

Problem

You would like to communicate with a server using a proto-col that is not directly supported by Adobe AIR (for exam-ple, communicate with an FTP server).

Solution

Use the Socket class in the AIR API to send binary or text data to the server and register for events that will alert you to incoming data from the server.

Discussion

When communicating using protocols other than those directly supported by Adobe AIR, you may need to use the Socket API. The Socket API is an asynchronous API that lets you send data to a persistent socket endpoint and receive data from it in real time. You do not need to create a new Socket instance for each set of data sent to the same endpoint. The connection can be kept alive for the entire conversation between your client and the service to which you're connecting. This is the typical flow when using the Socket API:

1. Create a connection to the endpoint
2. Listen for notification of connection success or failure
3. Queue data that will be sent to the endpoint
4. Send the data to the endpoint
5. Listen for data incoming from the endpoint
6. Repeat steps 3 through 5
7. Close the connection

The first step is to create a connection to the socket endpoint that consists of a host and a port number. For example, to connect to an endpoint the host might be 'foo.com' and the port number might be 5555. Create the instance of the Socket class and connect to the endpoint using that information. At this time, we will also set up our listeners to listen for the different events that the Socket can dispatch:

```
var socket = new air.Socket( );
socket.addEventListener( air.Event.CONNECT, onSocketOpen );
socket.addEventListener( air.ProgressEvent.SOCKET_DATA,
onSocketData );
socket.connect( 'foo.com', 5555 );
```

We will also need to create the functions to handle the events we subscribed for. The first event is the `air.Event.CONNECT` event. This event will tell us when the socket has been initiated and communication with the service behind the endpoint is possible. In this example, we are sending the bytes of a UTF-8 encoded string to the service:

```
function onSocketOpen( event )
{
    // This queues up the binary representation of the
    // string 'Bob' in UTF-8 format to be sent to the
```

```
        // endpoint.
        socket.writeUTFBytes( "Bob" );

        // Send the actual bytes to the server and clear
        // the stream. We then wait for data to be sent
        // back to us.
        socket.flush( );
    }
```

The `air.ProgressEvent.SOCKET_DATA` event is dispatched whenever data is received. The service we are connecting to uses a simple protocol: we send a UTF-8 encoded string and it returns a UTF-8 encoded string. This makes accessing the data sent back to us very simple. To access this data, we measure the total bytes of data available on the Socket and read that many bytes as a UTF-8 encoded string using the read `readUTFBytes( )` method of the Socket class.

```
    function onSocketData( event )
    {
        var data =
          socket.readUTFBytes( socket.bytesAvailable );
        air.trace( data ); // Hello Bob
    }
```

In our example, the protocol of communication was just a single string. In some cases, depending on the service with which you're communicating, you may need to send and receive other data types. The Socket class provides methods for reading and writing many data types, such as ints, Booleans, floats, etc. For example, if we were talking with a fictional service that required us to send a Boolean followed by an int, our `onSocketOpen` function in the above example could look like this:

```
    function onSocketOpen( event )
    {
        // First send the boolean
        socket.writeBoolean( true );
        // Now send an int
        socket.writeInt( 10 );
```

```
      // Now we send the bytes to the service and
      // clear the buffer.
      socket.flush();
}
```

This example provides a baseline of functionality that can be
expanded upon to speak to many different protocols. The
only current limitation is that there is not currently an SSL
Socket implementation in AIR. For secure communication
you will be limited to HTTPS:

```
<html>
<head>

<title>Communicating on a Socket</title>
<script type="text/javascript" src="AIRAliases.js">
</script>

<script>
var socket = null;

function init()
{
   socket = new air.Socket();

   // Create our listeners which tell us when the Socket
   // is open and when we receive data from our service.
    socket.addEventListener( air.Event.CONNECT, onSocketOpen );
    socket.addEventListener( air.ProgressEvent.SOCKET_DATA,
                             onSocketData );

   // Connect to our service, which is located at host foo.com
   // using port 5555.
   socket.connect( 'foo.com', 5555 );
}

function onSocketOpen( event )
{
   // This queues up the binary representation of the
   // string 'Bob' in UTF-8 format to be sent to the
   // endpoint.
   socket.writeUTFBytes( "Bob" );

   // Send the actual bytes to the server and clear
   // the stream. We then wait for data to be sent
```

```
    // back to us.
    socket.flush( );
}

function onSocketData( event )
{
    var data = socket.readUTFBytes( socket.bytesAvailable );
    air.trace( data ); // Hello Bob
}
</script>

</head>
<body onload="init( )">
</body>
</html>
```

Uploading a File in the Background

Problem

The application user has created numerous files offline, and you now want to send those to the server without blocking the user from doing any additional work.

Solution

The File class in Adobe AIR provides an upload( ) method that is designed specifically for this purpose, without having to create and manage HTML forms.

Discussion

The File.upload( ) method can upload files via HTTP/S to a server for additional processing. The upload takes places just like a traditional multipart file upload from an HTML form, but without the need to manipulate forms on the client. The upload process also takes place asynchronously in the background, allowing the application to continue processing without interruption.

The implementation of the receiving server is beyond the scope of this example. There are numerous technologies, and tutorials for these technologies, that elegantly handle file upload. You're encouraged to investigate your options.

The primary events that are useful are `ProgressEvent.PROGRESS` and `Event.COMPLETE`. These events handle notifying the application of upload progress, and when an individual upload is complete, respectively:

```
var file =
new air.File.documentsDirectory.resolve( "myImage.jpg" );

file.addEventListener( air.ProgressEvent.PROGRESS,
                       doProgress );
file.addEventListener( air.Event.COMPLETE, doComplete );
```

The `ProgressEvent` contains various properties that can help in reflecting upload progress in the user interface. The most notable of these properties are `ProgressEvent.byteLoaded` and `ProgressEvent.bytesTotal`, which show how much of the file has been uploaded and the total size of the file. The `Event.COMPLETE` is broadcast once the upload is complete.

To start the upload, you first need a valid File object that points to a resource on disk.

Once a valid file reference is established, developers will want to call the `File.upload( )` method. The `File.upload( )` method can take three arguments, the first of which is a `URLRequest` object that contains information about where the file should be sent. The `URLRequest` object can also contain additional data to be passed to the receiving server. This additional data manifests itself as HTML form fields might during a traditional multipart file upload:

```
var request = new air.URLRequest( "http://www.mydomain.
com/upload" );
file.upload( request, "image", false );
```

The second argument provided to the File.upload( ) method call is the name of the form field that contains the file data.

The third argument is a Boolean value that tells the upload process if it should try a test before sending the actual file. The test upload will POST approximately 10KB of data to the endpoint to see if the endpoint responds. If the service monitoring capabilities of the Adobe Integrated Runtime are not being used, this is a good way to check for potential failure of the process.

TIP

More than one great web application has been caught by this subtlety before. If the server is expecting the file data outright, then a test upload will almost assuredly cause an error. If you intend to use the test facility, be sure that your server code is prepared to handle the scenario.

```
function doProgress( event )
{
    var pct = Math.ceil( ( event.bytesLoaded / event.
bytesTotal ) * 100 );
    document.getElementById( "progress" ).innerText =
    pct + "%";
}
```

The Event.COMPLETE event is relatively straightforward in that it signals the completion of the upload process. This is a good place to perform any file system maintenance that might otherwise need to be accomplished by the application. An example would be removing the just-uploaded file from the local disk to free up space. Another task that might be accomplished in the Event.COMPLETE handler is to start the upload of subsequent files:

```
<html>
<head>

<title>Background Upload</title>
<script type="text/javascript" src="AIRAliases.js">
</script>
```

```
<script>
var file = null;

function doComplete()
{
    document.getElementById( "txtProgress" ).style.
      visibility = "hidden";
    document.getElementById( "txtProgress" ).innerText =
                             "Uploading... 0%";

    document.getElementById( "btnUpload" ).disabled =
     null;
}

function doLoad()
{
    file = air.File.documentsDirectory;
    file.addEventListener( air.Event.SELECT, doSelect );
    file.addEventListener( air.ProgressEvent.PROGRESS,
doProgress );
    file.addEventListener( air.Event.COMPLETE, doComplete
);

    document.getElementById( "btnUpload" ).
addEventListener( "click", doUpload );
}

function doProgress( event )
{
    var loaded = event.bytesLoaded;
    var total = event.bytesTotal;
    var pct = Math.ceil( ( loaded / total ) * 100 );

    document.getElementById( "txtProgress" ).innerText =
"Uploading... " + pct.toString() + "%";
}

function doSelect()
{
    var request =
    new air.URLRequest( "http://www.ketnerlake.com/work/
                        watcher/upload.cfm" );

    document.getElementById( "btnUpload" ).disabled =
                                      "disabled";
    document.getElementById( "txtProgress" ).style.
      visibility = "visible";
```

```
        file.upload( request, "image", false );
}

function doUpload()
{
        file.browseForOpen( "Select File" );
}
</script>

</head>
<body onload="doLoad()">

<input id="btnUpload" type="button" value="Upload" />

<div id="txtProgress" style="visibility: hidden">
Uploading... 0%</div>

</body>
</html>
```

Sound

Playing a Sound

Problem

You need to play a sound in your application.

Solution

Use the Sound API within AIR to play an MP3 file.

Discussion

AIR includes complete support for accessing Flash Player APIs from JavaScript. This includes the Sound class that can be used to play local or remote MP3 files.

Playing a sound is simple, and requires two main steps:

1. Create a URLRequest instance that references the local or remote sound.
2. Pass the URLRequest to the Sound instance, and play it.

Here is the relevant code snippet:

```
var soundPath =
  new air.URLRequest("app-resource:/sound.mp3");
var s = new air.Sound( );
    s.load(soundPath);
    s.play( );
```

First, we create a URLRequest that points to the location of the MP3 file we will play. In this case, we use an app-resource URI that references the *sound.mp3* file contained in the application install directory. You can also use any valid URI, including both file and http URIs:

```
var soundPath =
  new air.URLRequest("app-resource:/sound.mp3");
```

We then create an instance of the Sound class, pass the reference to the MP3 path, and then call play:

```
var s = new air.Sound( );
    s.load(soundPath);
    s.play( );
```

Here is the complete example with a play button:

```
<html>
<head>

    <script src="AIRAliases.js" />
    <script type="text/javascript">

        function playSound( )
        {
            var soundPath =
             new air.URLRequest("app-resource:/sound.mp3");
            var s = new air.Sound( );
                s.load(soundPath);
                s.play( );
        }
    </script>

</head>

<body>
    <input type="button" value="Play" onClick="playSound( )">
</body>
</html>
```

At this point, you should have a solid understanding of Adobe AIR, how to build AIR applications, and work with AIR APIs. Make sure to check the resources listed in the Preface to learn more advanced Adobe AIR development techniques.

AIR Command-Line Tools

The AIR SDK provides the following command-line tools:

ADL
> Use this tool to launch and test an AIR application without having to install it.

ADT
> Use this tool to package an AIR application into a redistributable AIR file.

This Appendix lists the options for each of the command-line tools.

For an example of using these tools, see Chapter 2.

ADL

ADL is a command-line tool that launches an AIR application, based on its application descriptor file, without requiring that the application be installed. This is useful for testing and debugging the application.

Typically, you want to call the ADL tool passing one parameter: the path to the application descriptor file (the application *.xml* file):

```
adl application.xml
```

The full syntax of the ADL command is:

```
adl ( -runtime <path-to-runtime-dir> )? <path-to-app-xml>
<path-to-root-dir>? ( -- ... )?
```

Table A-1 provides a description of the command-line arguments for ADL.

Table A-1. ADL command-line arguments

Option	Description
`-runtime`	Optional argument that specifies the directory that contains the AIR runtime that should be used.
`path-app-xml`	The application descriptor file for the application that should be launched.
`path-to-root-dir`	Optional argument that specifies the directory that contains the application descriptor file
`--`	Any arguments specified after this argument will be passed to the application as startup/command-line arguments, and can be accessed from the application via the InvokeEvent

ADT

ADT is a command-line tool that packages AIR applications into redistributable AIR files. AIR can then install the AIR application from that AIR file.

Typically, you want to call the ADT tool in the following way:

```
adt -package HelloWorld.air application.xml HelloWorld.swf
```

In this example, the ADT tool creates an AIR file named *HelloWorld.air* based on the *application.xml* application descriptor file.

The syntax of the ADT command is:

```
adt -package <air-file> <app-xml> <fileOrDir>* ( -C <dir>
<fileOrDir>+ )*
```

Table A-2 shows the command-line options for ADT.

Table A-2. Command-line options for ADT

Option	Description
-package	The first argument must be -package.
air-file	The relative or absolute path to the AIR to be created by ADT.
app-xml	The relative or absolute path to the application descriptor file for the application.
fileOrDir	One or more file or directory names identifying other files to be included in the package. Each successive file or directory name should be separated by a space. If a directory name is specified, then all of the files in that directory and its subdirectories will be included. However, files that are marked hidden in the file system will be ignored. If any of the files listed is the same as the file specified in the <app-xml> parameter, then it will be ignored; it will not be added to the package file a second time. These files and directories will be copied into the application install directory when the application is installed.
-C <dir>	This changes the root directory path for subsequent files or directories listed in the command line.

AIR JavaScript Aliases

Tables B-1 through B-12 show the JavaScript aliases created in *AIRAliases.js* and the AIR and Flash Player APIs to which they correspond.

TIP

All nonaliased ActionScript APIs are accessed through the window.runtime property in JavaScript.

Table B-1. Top-level aliases

Alias	ActionScript API
air.trace	trace
air.navigateToURL	flash.net.navigateToURL
air.sendToURL	flash.net.sendToURL

Table B-2. File aliases

Alias	ActionScript API
air.File	flash.filesystem.File
air.FileStream	flash.filesystem.FileStream
air.FileMode	flash.filesystem.FileMode

Table B-3. Event aliases

Alias	ActionScript API
air.Event	flash.events.Event
air.FileListEvent	flash.events.FileListEvent

Table B-3. Event aliases (continued)

Alias	ActionScript API
air.IOErrorEvent	flash.events.IOErrorEvent
air.InvokeEvent	flash.events.InvokeEvent
air.HTTPStatusEvent	flash.events.HTTPStatusEvent
air.SecurityErrorEvent	flash.events.SecurityErrorEvent
air.AsyncErrorEvent	flash.events.AsyncErrorEvent
air.NetStatusEvent	flash.events.NetStatusEvent
air.OutputProgressEvent	flash.events.OutputProgressEvent
air.ProgressEvent	flash.events.ProgressEvent
air.StatusEvent	flash.events.StatusEvent
air.EventDispatcher	flash.events.EventDispatcher
air.DataEvent	flash.events.DataEvent
air.TimerEvent	flash.events.TimerEvent

Table B-4. Native window aliases

Alias	ActionScript API
air.NativeWindow	air.NativeWindow = flash.display.NativeWindow
air.NativeWindowDisplayState	flash.display.NativeWindowDisplayState
air.NativeWindowInitOptions	flash.display.NativeWindowInitOptions
air.NativeWindowSystemChrome	flash.display.NativeWindowSystemChrome
air.NativeWindowResize	flash.display.NativeWindowResize
air.NativeWindowType	flash.display.NativeWindowType
air.NativeWindowErrorEvent	flash.events.NativeWindowErrorEvent
air.NativeWindowBoundsEvent	flash.events.NativeWindowBoundsEvent
air.NativeWindowDisplayStateEvent	flash.events.NativeWindowDisplayStateEvent

Table B-5. Geometry aliases

Alias	ActionScript API
air.Point	flash.geom.Point
air.Rectangle	flash.geom.Rectangle

Table B-6. Network aliases

Alias	ActionScript API
air.FileFilter	flash.net.FileFilter
air.LocalConnection	flash.net.LocalConnection
air.NetConnection	flash.net.NetConnection
air.URLLoader	flash.net.URLLoader
air.URLLoaderDataFormat	flash.net.URLLoaderDataFormat
air.URLRequest	flash.net.URLRequest
air.URLRequestDefaults	flash.net.URLRequestDefaults
air.URLRequestHeader	flash.net.URLRequestHeader
air.URLRequestMethod	flash.net.URLRequestMethod
air.URLStream	flash.net.URLStream
air.URLVariables	flash.net.URLVariables
air.Socket	air.Socket = flash.net.Socket
air.XMLSocket	flash.net.XMLSocket
air.Responder	flash.net.Responder
air.ObjectEncoding	flash.net.ObjectEncoding

Table B-7. System aliases

Alias	ActionScript API
air.Shell	flash.system.Shell
air.System	flash.system.System
air.Security	flash.system.Security
air.Updater	flash.system.Updater

Table B-8. Capabilities aliases

Alias	ActionScript API
air.Capabilities	flash.system.Capabilities
air.NativeWindowCapabilities	flash.system.NativeWindowCapabilities

Table B-9. Desktop aliases

Alias	ActionScript API
air.ClipboardManager	flash.desktop.ClipboardManager
air.TransferableData	flash.desktop.TransferableData
air.TransferableFormats	flash.desktop.TransferableFormats
air.TransferableTransferMode	flash.desktop.TransferableTransferMode

Table B-10. Utility aliases

Alias	ActionScript API
air.ByteArray	flash.utils.ByteArray
air.Dictionary	flash.utils.Dictionary
air.Endian	flash.utils.Endian
air.Timer	flash.utils.Timer

Table B-11. Media aliases

Alias	ActionScript API
air.ID3Info	flash.media.ID3Info
air.Sound	flash.media.Sound
air.SoundChannel	flash.media.SoundChannel
air.SoundLoaderContext	flash.media.SoundLoaderContext
air.SoundMixer	flash.media.SoundMixer
air.SoundTransform	flash.media.SoundTransform

Table B-12. SQL/Database aliases

Alias	ActionScript API
air.SQLConnection	flash.data.SQLConnection
air.SQLStatement	flash.data.SQLStatement
air.SQLResult	flash.data.SQLResult
air.SQLError	flash.errors.SQLError
air.SQLErrorEvent	flash.events.SQLErrorEvent
air.SQLErrorCode	flash.errors.SQLErrorCode
air.SQLEvent	flash.events.SQLEvent
air.SQLUpdateEvent	flash.events.SQLUpdateEvent
air.SQLTransactionLockType	flash.data.SQLTransactionLockType
air.SQLColumnNameStyle	flash.data.SQLColumnNameStyle
air.SQLErrorOperation	flash.errors.SQLErrorOperation

Index